Performing
Texts

P·E·R·F·O·R·M·I·N·G

T·E·X·T·S

EDITED BY

MICHAEL ISSACHAROFF

AND

ROBIN F. JONES

upp

UNIVERSITY OF PENNSYLVANIA PRESS

PHILADELPHIA

The publication of this volume was partially funded by a grant from the Office of the Dean, Faculty of Arts, University of Western Ontario. The University of Pennsylvania Press gratefully acknowledges this assistance.

Library of Congress Cataloging-in-Publication Data

Performing texts.
  "Essays . . . originally written for presentation at
an International Symposium on the Theory and Practice
of Performance "Scène, signe, spectacle", held under
the auspices of the Faculty of Arts and the French
Department of the University of Western Ontario in
April 1983"—
  Bibliography: p.
  Includes index.
  1. Theater—Congresses. I. Issacharoff, Michael.
II. Jones, Robin F. III. International Symposium on
Theory and Practice of Performance "Scène, signe,
spectacle" (1983 : University of Western Ontario)
PN2018.P47 1987   792   87-19769

ISBN 8-8122-8073-3

Contents

Acknowledgments
vii

Introduction
MICHAEL ISSACHAROFF and ROBIN F. JONES
1

The Mystery of the Play Experience: Quince's Questions
J. L. STYAN
9

Self-Referring Artifacts
ANNA WHITESIDE
27

Much Ado About Doing Things With Words (and Other Means):
Some Problems in the Pragmatics of Theatre and Drama
KEIR ELAM
39

Stage Codes
MICHAEL ISSACHAROFF
59

Decoding Mnouchkine's Shakespeare (A Grammar of Stage Signs)
JEAN ALTER
75

From Text to Performance
PATRICE PAVIS
86

A Medieval Prescription for Performance (*Le Jeu d'Adam*)
ROBIN F. JONES
101

Performance Orientations in Ritual Theatre
RICHARD SCHECHNER
116

Postscript or Pinch of Salt: Performance as Mediation or
Deconstruction
MICHAEL ISSACHAROFF
138

Bibliography
145

Contributors
153

Index
155

Acknowledgments

The essays in this volume were originally written for presentation at an international Symposium on the Theory and Practice of Performance ("Scène, Signe, Spectacle"), held under the auspices of the Faculty of Arts and the French Department of the University of Western Ontario in April 1983. All the essays have been revised for publication.

Financial support for the conference was generously provided by the Cultural Services of the French Embassy in Ottawa, The British Council (through the British High Commission in Ottawa), the Social Sciences and Humanities Research Council of Canada, and the University of Western Ontario. It is a particular pleasure to record our thanks here.

We also want to thank M. Etienne Wermester, attaché culturel auprès du Consulat de France, Toronto; Charles Chadwick, representative, The British Council, Ottawa, for support and warm encouragement when the conference was still in the planning stage; Nancy Stotts-Jones for timely help with the typing of the manuscript; and Zachary Simpson, our editor at the University of Pennsylvania Press, for his support.

Introduction

MICHAEL ISSACHAROFF and ROBIN F. JONES

The title *Performing Texts* is intentionally polysemous. It can be taken to mean texts intended for performance, how to perform texts, or texts that themselves perform. "Texts" could be taken to mean the text of a play written by an author, the text of the director who has worked on the author's script and annotated it for his or her production, or the performance itself, understood as a language of sound, light, and movement, to be interpreted by the audience. The reach of meaning of the title is justified by our topic, which is the dynamic relation between script and performance, performance and reception.

The relation of text to performance is discussed by Patrice Pavis ("From Text to Performance"), Robin F. Jones ("A Medieval Prescription for Performance"), Michael Issacharoff ("Stage Codes") and even Richard Schechner ("Performance Orientations in Ritual Theatre")—despite his corpus of unscripted performances (*Ramlila* and *Yaqui Easter*)—if performance, inscribed in ritual, can be equated with regular theatre text. The nature of performance together with its relation to reception is discussed by John Styan ("The Mystery of the Play Experience"), Anna Whiteside ("Self-Referring Artifacts"), Jean Alter ("Decoding Mnouchkine's Shakespeare"), Keir Elam ("Much Ado About Doing Things with Words"), and, if one emphasizes the enactment of ritual (rather than its prescriptive force, as above), by Schechner. But *Performing Texts* is more than a binary exploration of the text/performance dichotomy. The richness of the collection lies, at least in part, with the reader, who, like the reader of Marc Saporta's novel, *Composition No. 1* or Gustave Flaubert's *Trois Contes*, or the performer of Pierre Boulez's Third Piano Sonata, is free to choose not

1

only the order, but also the emphasis and the arrangement, of the chapters that follow.

• • •

The theoretical study of theatre in the twentieth century can be traced back to the Prague School, whose major figures include Mukarovsky, Bogatyrev, Zich, Honzl, Brusak, and Veltrusky. Its history is much longer, of course, going all the way back to Aristotle and the *Poetics.* Current interest, parallel to the increased research activity in literary theory, particularly prevalent in Europe and North America in the last twenty years, has been growing rapidly. (See the bibliography at the end of this volume.) Fields of recent inquiry range from performance theory (especially semiotic and anthropological), dramatic speech act theory, and reception theory (informed by semiotics), to semiotics and deconstruction. Three volumes published in the last ten years have had a crucial impact: Anne Ubersfeld's *Lire le théâtre* (1977), Elam's *The Semiotics of Drama and Theatre* (1980), and the special 1981 issue of *Poetics Today* ("Drama, Theater, Performance. A Semiotic Perspective"). All three place special emphasis on the semiotics of the script or of the script in performance. Of these fields (some of which overlap), it is semiotics (script/performance), performance, and reception theory that privilege the characteristics peculiar to the medium of drama. Performance is not created *ex nihilo.* It is contingent on a text (however that term is understood), and the *process* whereby this text is forged and offered for reception as a performance deserves exploration. Hence the twin focus of our collection and indeed our title.

The contributors to this collection would agree with John Styan that the theatre is a process of communication and that "the audience makes its contribution to the creation of the play by its interpretation of the signs and signals [on the stage]." Styan confesses, however, that he is what Barthes called a "semioclast," and that for him the mystery of the play experience "would seem to close out rational discussion and even inhibit the use of semiotics." His position is that the mystery itself is what is transacted between actors and the audience, that this transaction, ever-changing, like audiences themselves, eludes any attempt at codification or systematization. Understandably, therefore, Styan's interest is in whole, individual live performances rather than in performance theory, which takes as its corpus aspects of performance, live or otherwise. And yet the study of what happens on the stage, which Styan recommends, must begin somewhere, failing which, the mystery is bound to remain a mystery.

Styan is of course right to insist on the primacy of live performance, yet what strategies are available for *studying* this ephemeral and elusive phenomenon? The most obvious place to start would seem to be the stage directions that are at least a permanent trace of performance, albeit virtual. In any case, the priority and value of the live performance over that which a reader may conjure up is a moot point; for purposes of critical scrutiny both are mediated by a text, for the live performance survives only thanks to the critic who speaks of it, and likewise the performance imagined and then expressed by the reader.

On the issue of stage directions, however, opinion is divided. Pavis and Elam reject authorial constraint, expressed by the didascalia, and it is useful to characterize their positions. Pavis valorizes the historical context and consequently subordinates the author's voice to that of the *metteur en scène*. Elam, taking issue with John Searle, sees in privileging didascalia the risk of downgrading the dialogue that, however, is the only verbal channel to survive in performance.

If it is not a requirement that the organization of materials used in dramatic representation follow the author's wishes, what is the relationship that joins the written word and its stage performance? For Pavis it is a function of the *mise en scène* that he describes as a metatext or commentary, disseminated throughout the various nonverbal channels (gesture, movement, configuration, rhythm, costume, lighting) but forged into a system and apparent only at the moment of performance. This commentary is arrived at conventionally enough through dramaturgical analysis, but though inspired by the text, it does not aspire to give it form by converting or translating it into a corresponding language of performance. The mise en scène is not the stage equivalent of the dramatic text, but rather is a prism designed to color perception of the verbal channel in performance. The mise en scène is therefore an act of mediation, or more precisely a "contextualized" (i.e., historically staged) reading of the dialogue, with overdetermination, irony, and contradiction as its most obvious and fertile modes of exploitation. As a basic typology, Pavis proposes the following categories: the autotextual—the mise en scène supports the internal logic of the playscript, its narrative architecture; the ideotextual—the text as an aesthetic object is subverted by the ideas and the social context it is made to articulate; the intertextual—the mise en scène mediates between the structure of the text and ideological reference, renewing the text in response to the contemporary social context and in relation to other, past performances.

The theory and definition of mise en scène proposed by Pavis clearly rely on a dialectic of the nonverbal with a text that survives the transformation of dramatic representation and remains referentially potent on stage. It is not surprising, therefore, that he chooses to illustrate his discussion of the relationship of mise en scène and the dramatic text with references to traditional, logocentric theatre, that of Marivaux. In much contemporary theatre, however, the verbal channel may disappear altogether or may simply survive as play, emptied of referential power; the polarization of the multiple channels of dramatic performance as text and gloss, verbally conveyed meaning and nonverbal commentary is consequently lost. In such theatre, the nonverbal no longer automatically functions as an exegetical frame to be constantly revamped in step with an historically evolving concretization of a text and is thus much less likely to attract the creative and interpretive revisions of the metteur en scène.

Starting from much the same position as Pavis, namely that the metteur en scène is always free to leave unfulfilled the dramatist's speech acts, Elam asks what words actually "do" in the so-called fictional universe of the drama, when they are issued under the authority of the actor. He argues that what the actor in fact "does," is to use the stage as his vehicle rather than confine himself to the locutionary act—that is, to the role of the empty vessel making noises.

If the actor, in Elam's estimation, may be said to be speaking on his own account (taking his own part), what is he communicating? Using Barthes's *punctum/studium* dichotomy, Elam suggests semiotizing the *punctum*. He relates Barthes's terms to Austin's perlocutionary function, for him the quintessential theatrical communication process, and establishes a further link between it and Aristotle's notion of catharsis or purgation. Finally, Elam places the perlocutionary function within the historical tradition dating back to the Aristotelian idea of the impact of performance on the audience, or catharsis, in its turn related to the theories of Horace, Scaliger, Sidney, and, of course, Artaud. For Elam, then, the basis of theatre pragmatics should be precisely the business of pathos: what counts, he maintains, is actor-audience interaction, which, he argues, is the principal force of post-Artaudian drama. As he aptly puts it, "every word stabs."

Elam's position is suggestive. It rescues drama from the passive category of display discourse, bringing it closer to an *activist* perspective, thereby emphasizing its impact as well as its subversive potential. In so doing, Elam's standpoint is not far removed from that of some Marxist theorists, such as Anne Ubersfeld, with their emphasis not so much, perhaps, on the emotional thrust of a performance as on its ideological implications. As Sartre had it, even to reveal the world, as the writer does by talking about it, is after all, to change it.

But are stage directions (as potential speech acts) to be dismissed quite as unreservedly as Pavis and Elam propose? Should authorial instructions be rejected out of hand? They are not necessarily confined to the italicized portion of the script (the didascalia). The dialogue often contains embedded signals essential for performance. The twelfth-century Anglo-Norman *Jeu d'Adam* (Jones) provides an extreme example of control intended through didascalia, comparable to Beckett's *Act Without Words* in which, significantly, it is the dialogue for once that is displaced by the author's instructions. The medieval prescription for performance is in complete contrast to Shakespeare's plays, which are perhaps the prime example of a discursive convention in which didascalia are kept to a minimum; information pertinent to the staging of the play is inscribed in the dialogue, rather than separated from it and given as distinct authorial directives.

Yet stage directions can be seen as one of the major forces contributing to the cohesion of the dramatic script. This, at any rate, is the position taken by Michael Issacharoff. Textual cohesion is described as the interlocking of dramatic codes, which may be directly recommended by the author or distilled from the dialogue. Clear examples of cohesion are provided by an albeit simplified dramatic medium— radio drama. Since the visual channel is not used in radio plays, cohesion is likely to be greater, as the visual, décor for example, is conveyed by sound. Time, rather than space, becomes the crucial dimension. Simultaneity is contingent on the visual; radio drama, however, tends to privilege linearity in order to avoid overloading its single informational channel. Everything in radio plays must happen audibly. Accordingly, all systems in such plays are linked to sound. Any system, costume, gesture, and so forth must be transformed into a verbal cue, whereas décor, similarly, must be expressed through sound effects, or through a verbal reference in the dialogue. Consequently, sound may mean space, movement, gesture, or even time itself.

Code focus in radio drama is greater than in any other type of theatre, since everything that happens is subordinate to two modes: voice and nonvoice. Both hinge on consecutive (and thus linear) rather than on simultaneous (and thus nonlinear) presentation. Radio drama demonstrates not only explicit linkage between the various systems at work but also the presence of a clearly articulated hierarchy.

Whether the performance is constructed according to the author's instructions or relies on a set substituted for them by the metteur en scène, the process of *becoming* ceases, on stage, to have any relevance. In performance, emphasis shifts, of necessity, to communication—that is, to the charge of meaning borne by the various channels and the way in which they combine to guide reception. Sound, in which code cohesion is anchored in radio drama, yields precedence in regular drama to space, the constraints of which, as Elam has observed, "remain the primary influence on perception and reception." In this respect, Jones's paper is closely related to Schechner's on ritual theatre in India and Arizona. Both papers discuss the semiotization of scenography and the configuration and orientation of stage materials in relation to performance meaning and audience reception.

Jones's and Schechner's examples exploit a multiple set, composed of several play stations, to and from which the actors move in the course of the dramatic action. In performance, stations function both as distinct locations and as combinations of places having a particular design and orientation. In the *Adam,* the topography of the set, the physical features of which are foregrounded verbally, kinetically, and proxemically, as well as by vestimentary codes, is linked topologically to the four cardinal points of the compass and to the values with which medieval Christendom had invested them. Space, semiotized by association and convention, thus becomes a low-level source of meaning and a tacit means of controlling perception. As such, just as the verbal channel it houses is subject to commentary by the mise en scène, it too is subject to glossing in a reversal of the function attributed by Pavis to the nonverbal. In the *Adam,* the meanings with which the set is infused by convention are both confirmed and redefined by language. The latter process is apparent in the extensive application of feudal terminology to the relationship between God and man; Eden is referred to both as earthly paradise and as Adam's fief, for example. Viewed from this perspective, it might be contended that the conventional sense of the set, contributed by the social and philosophical context, is here being redirected by verbal commentary and channeled into service as a vehicle for the parasitical expression of the interests of the feudal nobility.

For Schechner, too, performance space is a performing component of theatre, speaking a language of configuration derived from local and national geography and charged with mythic and historical meaning. In Ramlila of Ramnagar, for example, the set (the town and its environs used as a stage) is a more or less accurate model of India and Sri Lanka. Consequently, in performance, the play stations exist in superimposed narrative and existential frames, as texts in a palimpsest, triggering meanings through a process of mutual reflection; heroic exploits take place simultaneously in a mythic and an actual India. Environmental theatre of the sort described by Schechner provides an exaggerated illustration of the circuit connecting text, stage, and audience, an enlarged model for the discussion of theatre.

The staging described by Jones and Schechner is consistent with authority, be it that vested in a text or in ritual and topography, which operate in Ramlila and Yaqui Easter as implied didascalia. If performances of this sort enhance communication or celebration, Alter's paper exemplifies the other extreme. He describes Mnouchkine's *Richard II*, staged in the kabuki style, in which the highly conventionalized system of traditional Japanese stage signs provided the context of utterance for the Elizabethan verbal channel, delivered, in French translation, in a manner worthy of the Comédie-Française. One recalls an earlier production of Shakespeare in the Japanese style, Gordon McDougall and Misturu Ishii's *Tempest* at Oxford and Cambridge in 1976, currently playing (as of February 1986) in an updated version at Edmonton's Citadel Theatre in Canada. While recognizing that on stage the verbal channel becomes one of many sets of stage signs, Alter distinguishes the text from the other performance or performing channels by reason of its special referential power. Alter contends that in Shakespeare, kabuki style, the unusual marriage of verbal and performant signs is not a harmonious one: rather than complement each other, the figurative and the symbolic, the verbal and the performant, compete for attention and thus exhaust their referential energies through conflict—not in generating a harmonious totality of meaning, but in self-reference, in show. The signs refer to themselves as aesthetic process. The self-reflexive, self-conscious performance is especially fertile for exploration of the mechanics of theatre, its theatricality. For Alter, it is also the sign of cultural tensions, alienation from reality, the herald of an age in which signs refer only to other signs in a mirroring process that promotes the power to mean rather than meaning itself.

The self-referential mode disrupts communication, undermining the theatre's potential for meaning. Defining reference both as the relationship between signifier and referent and as the process or act of referring, Whiteside explores the issue in relation to props and décor, characters and action, stage and audience. The sign, it is suggested, has an ambivalent status in drama, being at once both sign and referent. As in Ionesco, it may be alternately mentioned and allowed to foreground itself independently of the dialogue. Used in this way, signs such as the flaming horse's mane in *Jacques ou la soumission,* or the striking clock in *La Cantatrice chauve* acquire an additional function, that of referring to the theatrical medium itself. Theatre refers to itself as theatre, then, not only when the mise en scène is pried free from the author's control (Pavis), cut loose from the social context of the playscript, with cultural systems deliberately set at odds (as in Mnouchkine's *Richard II*), but also because in theatre the sign is always focused more or less sharply on its own materiality (the grain and texture of the spoken word, the paths of movement, the geometry of gesture, the play of light and color). In theatre, the referent *is* the performance or the conventions of the genre.

•   •   •

The papers that follow share a preoccupation with performance, yet they necessarily confront the text and, by implication, the authority that attempts to shape, govern, and channel. That text may be the author's playscript, the "text" developed by the director (the mise en scène), or the text established by ritual. It is this element of authority that, in the end, binds text to production, production to reception, from the tyranny of the Word of the sacred playscript to the subversion of the text as the repository of stable meaning. On stage, authority frames the transaction with the audience, for is it not the play on conventions, the respect or transgression of the hallowed space of performance and the common bounds of illusion, that open and close the distance between stage and auditorium, heighten or dissolve the sense of mystery, and make believe or transform stage acts into spectacle?

The Mystery of the Play Experience: Quince's Questions

J. L. STYAN

Dramatic semioticians are aware of the ripples they are causing in the classrooms and workshops across the country. Some kind of analytical tool has long been needed to enable us to talk about what an audience perceives on the stage, how it perceives it, and how the perception is translated into a conception. Though he would probably hate to be called a semiotician, John Russell Brown was right to emphasize years ago that a play reader is a different animal from a playgoer and that his or her perceptions will therefore very likely be different. More recently, Patrice Pavis was right to remind us that the relationship between text and performance is not one of simple implication but rather what he calls "dialectical," whereby the actor comments on and argues with the text[1]; some years ago, I found myself suggesting that Shakespeare's text prompted a "controlled freedom" of improvization for the actor.[2] In other fields, Keir Elam and others are right to find our ways of regarding the use of scene and costume, space and light, too impressionistic: we need to know more about how these features are defined by conventional patterns, social behavior, or aesthetic rules.

Above all, we must emphasize how important it is to understand the theatre as a process of communication, one that insists that the audience make its contribution to the creation of the play by interpreting the signs and signals from the stage, where everything seen and heard must acquire the strength of convention. Norman Rabkin, another Shakespearean, summed up the matter when he urged that we must learn to talk about "the process of our involvement rather than our considered view after the aesthetic event."[3] The previous emphasis of literary and dramatic criticism on what words "say" and not on how they say it has often rendered our thinking about plays and performances misleading or irrelevant, and those of us who were determined to train our students to use their eyes and ears found ourselves improvizing some kind of "play computer" designed to help us look in the "right" places. The right places increasingly were on the stage itself, where textual signals were to be interpreted by the players, and in the auditorium, where the final response to the play in performance could be found and examined. The problem was to do this without destroying the fabric of the play, without (to use Wordsworth's tidy phrase) being guilty of "murdering to dissect."

Nevertheless, while we assert the importance of understanding the process of drama and performance, some of the ripples we have caused are those of distrust. It would be dishonest of us not to acknowledge the considerable concern over the speed with which semiotic analysis and performance theory are moving into university campuses. At bottom, the question being asked is whether it is sensible to jettison fifty years of dramatic criticism, or what claimed to be dramatic criticism. At the very least, should the precious years of study not be spent in reading and performing the plays themselves? The controversy is somewhat reminiscent of when "new criticism" took hold in the 1940s and 1950s (and, incidentally, did so much harm to the study of drama and theatre, with which the new criticism could not cope). At my own university, students are conscious of a certain pressure to give time to semiotics lest they be left behind in the academic race, and complaints of intellectual blackmail are being heard.

This essay is first, therefore, a modest plea for us to respect our limitations. Like the human sciences of economics, sociology, anthropology, history, linguistics, psychology, and no doubt other semi-sciences, semiotics must always fall short of its goals. In the case of a creative and performing art like drama, to try to reduce to rule an art form that is so unpredictable, always growing and changing, so infinitely variable, must be frustrated, especially when so few dare claim to be masters of the medium and its best products. It will never be easy to propose a theory about Shakespeare's signs and signals when we are still a long way from knowing what his plays are capable of. This must also be true of a less romantic playwright like Racine. The history of poetic criticism is strewn with those who have tried to number the streaks of Samuel Johnson's tulip (*Rasselas*, Book 10). I should spell this out more clearly, and perhaps we could agree to identify four pitfalls that await the novice semiotician of drama and the theatre.

Pitfall 1: semiotics may try to make a science of art. We are alerted to this by such devices as the numbering of paragraphs and the listing of precedents in the best legal manner, as though what someone has said before somehow confirms what is being said now (a besetting sin among critics, one that I have already committed three or four times in this essay alone). Samuel Beckett saw the funny side of it when he had Lucky list his authorities in *Waiting for Godot:* Puncher and Wattmann, Testew and Cunard, Popov and Belcher. We do not blanch at turning to algebraic abstractions elements in the play that are themselves abstractions to begin with, creating only a shadow of a shadow, a skeleton of a skeleton. Some, like Wilfried Passow, find it the "duty" of theatre research "to try every conceivable approach to analyze presentation."[4] Others, like Patrice Pavis, are less sure: "Whatever the system of notation used, it is readily acknowledged that the notation of the performance simplifies it to the point of impoverishment."[5]

Pitfall 2: semiotics tends to abuse language in the name of communication. I cannot be alone in finding that reading semiotics constitutes one of our unhappiest reading experiences. It is tempting to quote a few lines, but this is unnecessary. Whole paragraphs, whole pages build one abstraction upon another to add up to a rarer and rarer meaninglessness, the higher blather. Much of the time it is simply a case of bad writing, an insensitivity to language that ill becomes a dramatic critic. At its worst, it can be an academic smoke screen thick with jargon and coinages. A word will be especially favored if it ends in *-ality* or *-icity,* like theatrality and theatricity, corporality and motoricity, gesturality and iconicity, spatiality and facticity. Dictionaries have been written to deal with the flood of new meanings. Each of us, of course, will have his or her own aversion: I have a personal dislike for "global" when "everywhere" will serve, and for "didascalia" where we used to say "stage directions."

Pitfall 3: semiotics can evade the experience of drama while seeming to confront it. It is possible to read many pages, even entire chapters and articles, and never see a mention of a play or a player, a playwright or an artist, as though the actuality of drama and theatre, the business of performance, might at a touch destroy a house of cards. There is a kind of purity in this position, but in adopting such

a distant manner, dramatic semiotics may well deny its own concern
for the teaching, practice, and appreciation of the art of drama, encouraging its students to turn away from the stage. It has always been
easier to talk about characters without mentioning players and to discuss drama without acknowledging the theatre: such has been the
practice in departments of literature for years. It would be a pity if
departments of drama and theatre now fell into such an old trap.
Keir Elam lately has pointed out that each theatrical signal "has (or
supposedly has) an 'aesthetic' justification," and it is still our duty to
discover what the signal contributes to the aesthetic experience.[6]

Pitfall 4: semiotics may presuppose knowledge of what is as yet unknown. The fundamental business of coming to grips with a creative
work has not necessarily been accomplished merely by assembling for
analysis the signs, codes, and systems that seem to be most appropriate to the case in hand. Such a practice may leap over the unknowns of the great dramatic moments, perhaps the real source of a
particular experience in the theatre, when it is these very unknowns
that we essentially seek to know. Who can account for the pleasure we
take in watching tragedy? Or explain Johnson's notion that if delusion
be admitted, it can have no certain limitation? Or the phenomenon
remarked by Jacques Copeau, that as soon as his stage filled with actors it disappeared? It may be that traditional Anglo-American prag-
matism, with its deep distrust of the higher blather and its vague
ideological approach to the arts, will still carry some validity. With all
the notation in the world, our chief task remains as before: to assess
how a play "works" (one jargon word I will allow).

As I was writing, I found myself concocting some devilish examination for those who would presume too much in offering to analyze
what goes on in performance. The exam might read like this:

Identify the signs and codify the elements of theatrical communication,
and attempt a simple dramatological analysis of the following problems:

1. When Oedipus proposed marriage to Jocasta, a woman many years
his senior, how did he not suspect that she might be his mother?

2. Identify the mixture of laughter and fear induced in the audience
by enacting the stage direction in Shakespeare's The Winter's Tale, "Exit
pursued by a bear."

3. When the totally incompetent policeman Dogberry is put in charge
of the apprehension and trial of the criminals in Shakespeare's Much Ado
about Nothing, why does the audience feel quite reassured that their victim Hero will come to no possible harm?

4. How can we tolerate three acts of Norwegian rain as it falls on the melancholy scenes of Oswald's decline to imbecility in Ibsen's *Ghosts* without being told whether his mother gives him the poison or not?

5. In *The Importance of Being Earnest*, how can we laugh uncontrollably at the appearance of Jack Worthing dressed in mourning for his brother?

6. Is it possible to explain why, in Chekhov's *The Cherry Orchard*, we deplore, rather than applaud, the sale of the orchard to Lopahin, when his wretched ancestors, as serfs, had given their blood for its survival?

These and a thousand other other theatrical mysteries have one factor in common, one that haunts all performance theory: they all arise from the hardly explicable act of drama itself. They arise from the strange urge on the part of the actor and the spectator during performance to share an experience, and it is this bond between stage and audience that supplies the key to our interpretation of the text at the moment when it is transcended by performance. Notions of the relationship between stage and audience go back to classical times. Certainly it was always in Shakespeare's mind that his audience should "Piece out our imperfections with your thoughts," not only in *Henry V* but also in every play he wrote, and notions of a "theatre contract" attributed recently to Klaus Lazarowicz and others are to be found in some form or other in every major commentary that has offered a view of the phenomenon of drama.

In the English tradition, it is amusing to read how concerned John Dryden was in 1672

> to raise the imagination of the audience, and to persuade them, for the time, that what they behold in the theatre is really performed. The poet is then to endeavour an absolute dominion over the minds of the spectators; for, though our fancy will contribute to its own deceit, yet a writer ought to help its operation.[7]

Unfortunately, in *The Conquest of Granada,* from whose prefatory essay I take.this passage, Dryden tried to help the fancy with an overabundance of drums and trumpets and stage battles, together with extravagant heroes and all the tropes and figures of an inflated rhetoric.

Samuel Johnson's 1765 defense of Shakespeare turns on a series of astonishing paradoxes:[8]

1. It is false, that any representation is mistaken for reality; that any dramatic fable in its materiality was ever credible, or, for a single moment, was ever credited.

2. If the spectator can be persuaded that his old acquaintances are Alexander and Caesar . . . he is in a state of elevation above the reach of reason.

3. The truth is, that the spectators are always in their senses, and know, from the first act to the last, that the stage is only a stage, and that the players are only players.

4. It will be asked, how the drama moves, if it is not credited. It is credited with all the credit due to a drama.

5. The delight of tragedy proceeds from our consciousness of fiction; if we thought murders and treasons real, they would please no more.

We are rather more romantic than this in the twentieth century. When Meyerhold discussed the productions of *The Death of Tintagiles* and *Pelléas and Mélisande* in Moscow in 1907, he claimed that "a performance of Maeterlinck is a mystery," emphasizing the word and using it in the sense of a religious rite. The idea of a bond between actor and spectator then fired his imagination, and he went on to discuss what happens when the actor is "left alone, face to face with the spectator." Words seemed to defeat him when he stated that, as a result of the friction between "the actor's creativity and the spectator's imagination" there is a union of "souls," of "unadulterated elements," so that "a clear flame is kindled."[9]

We continue to indulge in mysticism in our own time. Jean Giraudoux wrote enigmatically of the theatre as something more than simple "communication": for him, it was close to "communion." A play is received by an audience, he thought, as an act of love is, instinctively.[10]

The British director Tyrone Guthrie falls back on the concept of ritual:

> I believe that the theatre makes its effect not by means of illusion, but by ritual. People do not believe that what they see or hear on the stage is "really" happening. Action on the stage is a stylized re-enactment of real action, which is then imagined by the audience.[11]

Indeed, he likened an audience to a congregation in a church where participation in the ritual should leave it "rapt, literally 'taken out of itself,' to the extent that it shares the emotion which the priest or actor is suggesting."[12] Anne Righter had a comparable explanation for the way in which medieval drama worked and claimed that "[w]hile the performance lasted, audience and actors shared the same ritual world, a world more real than the one which existed outside its frame."[13] When, more recently, Passow reminded us that "a performance must be considered as a collaboration between actors and audience" and went on to use such slippery words as "cooperation," "collusion," and "participation," he is being no less romantic and mysterious.[14]

I for one cannot explain it. When an actor seems to act out my thoughts and feelings, we share some unpredictable act of giving and taking. All we can agree, perhaps, is that there must be a real actor and a real audience, both actual and not merely implied. Thereafter, no formal or abstract approach to text or performance will truly illuminate the enigma, no amount of "semanticization" of the dialogue, the "didascalia," or the "scenic elements" like bodies, setting, props, and costumes. The object of criticism must be the total performance, visual and aural, manipulating human space and time, working as performance in its due process in conditions of theatre. If the uncomfortable and distracting word *mystery* seems to close out rational discussion and even inhibit the use of semiotics, it nevertheless points to the aesthetic element we should attend to and not ignore.

I have now adopted the role of what Roland Barthes would call a "semioclast," and this may be a naughty moment to look at the way in which Peter Quince is used by Shakespeare to have his little meta-theatrical joke with his audience about its curious participation in his comedy *A Midsummer Night's Dream.* Quince is a carpenter by trade and by conviction, and an unusual example of an Elizabethan director and an early dramaturg. He seems to support Johnson's contention about delusion and its odd effect of having no certain limitations. It could also be that, through Quince, Shakespeare was declaring his own interest in theatrical semiotics. Like the Greeks, he always had a word for it, and it may be that some of his answers are to be found in a wood near Athens.

You will remember that Quince's men plan to produce the tragedy of Pyramus and Thisbe but are faced with some ponderous problems of performance. It is nearly at the midpoint of the play when the mechanicals begin their rehearsals in good earnest, long after Shakespeare himself has overcome his own problems of creating magic in the moonlight. Bottom is evidently worried by the possible reception of *Pyramus and Thisbe,* and particularly by the way the ladies in the audience may take it: "There are things in this comedy of Pyramus and Thisbe that will never please. First, Pyramus must draw a sword to kill himself; which the ladies cannot abide."[15] (3.1.8–10) Luckily, the matter is quickly resolved: they will write a prologue to say that Pyramus did not really kill himself. And Bottom adds, "for the more better assurance, tell them that I, Pyramus, am not Pyramus but Bottom the weaver: this will put them out of fear." If that is a questionable conclusion, Shakespeare has reminded us that Quince and Company are only actors, spirits of Prospero who will melt into thin air.

Then Snout, not usually known for his intelligence, makes a good, logical point: "Will not the ladies be afeared of the lion?" After further deep debate, the only solution they can think of is *another* prologue for Lion:

> You must name his name, and half his face must be seen through the lion's neck, and he himself must speak through, saying thus, and to the same defect: "Ladies," or "Fair ladies—I would wish you," or "I would request you," or "I would entreat you, not to fear, not to tremble: my life for yours. If you think I come hither as a lion, it were pity of my life. No: I am no such thing: I am a man as other men are. (3.1.35–43)

It is comforting, even surprising, to know that Snug is a man as other men are, but a whole play made up of prologues is unthinkable. When does a convention cease to be a convention? At some point, drama must be done and be seen to be done.

The next dramaturgical difficulty is more subtle; it has to do with the imaginative suspension of disbelief. Shakespeare's lines may speak for themselves:

> QUINCE: But there is two hard things: that is, to bring the moonlight into a chamber; for you know, Pyramus and Thisbe meet by moonlight.
>
> SNOUT: Doth the moon shine that night we play our play?
>
> BOTTOM: A calendar, a calendar! Look in the almanac; find out moonshine, find out moonshine!
>
> QUINCE: Yes, it doth shine that night.
>
> BOTTOM: Why, then may you leave a casement of the great chamber window, where we play, open; and the moon may shine in at the casement.
>
> QUINCE: Ay; or else one must come in with a bush of thorns and a lantern, and say he comes to disfigure or to present the person of Moonshine.
>
> (3.1.45–57)

Quince raises a fundamental question for the theatre. To imitate reality, does one try for realism, hoping for Mother Nature's cooperation, even in an English summer? Snout the slow-witted and Bottom the overconfident are here the realists: "Look in the almanac; find out moonshine." But Quince is not so sure of Bottom's realism—he must have tried putting on a play with the new realism before. He comes up with a more reliable method, the new symbolism: someone must come in "to disfigure, or to present, the person of Moonshine." That sounds more reasonable, though in the event, as you will remember, Starveling makes a rather thickheaded Moonshine, so heavily symbolic with a thorn bush and a lantern and a little dog and a stool to stand on, that the muddle he gets into is a hopelessly realistic one.

Nevertheless, we almost need to be reminded of the basic joke, that the play itself has been solving similar problems for two acts with no trouble at all. How did it do it? The Elizabethan audience did not doubt for a moment that it was only a play. If only Quince had been able to slip into Shakespeare's audience and see the opening scenes! Perhaps Pirandello's Quince would have asked his questions of the playwright himself. But wait: even if we agree that the spectators are always in their senses, is this true of a character? Is a character in a play supposed to know that he is in a play? This is altogether a new proposition, one advanced by Lionel Abel in his stimulating book *Metatheatre*, where he argued that Hamlet is a character "with an acute awareness of what it means to be staged."[16] If we can be persuaded that our old acquaintances are Alexander and Caesar, we may accept the idea that Quince was aware of himself as an inferior Shakespeare. Of course, Hamlet was concerned from the start about how the plot was going to work out, and at the end he dies before he knows ("I cannot live to hear the news from England," he says). What a pity Hamlet did not have Quince's freedom to adapt his own play: he could have brought in Fortinbras earlier and the play could have ended happily.

So Quince's questions are fundamental to the nature of theatre, and I would suggest that, though some plays are more obviously metatheatrical and self-conscious than others, there has never been a period when a good playwright did not exploit the audience's pliability, its readiness to believe. It is said that human beings are the only animals that can feel sympathy or see a joke; add to this that human beings are the only animals that go to the theatre. Perhaps these things are connected. But what do we find at the theatre? An extraordinary world indeed. For people hardly ever kill their fathers and marry their mothers or consult witches before deciding on a course of action. Why commit a robbery over a piece of paste jewelry? How can someone die of a wound oozing tomato ketchup? Yet these things we are asked to accept in the name of drama.

There are many stories of honest citizens who have been quite confounded by the world of the theatre. When Tom Jones took Partridge to see Garrick playing Hamlet, he asked him which actor was best. Tom was surprised to get the reply, "The King, without doubt." But did he not admire Garrick in the scene with the Ghost? "Pooh," said the honest Partridge, "I could act as well myself if I'd seen a ghost." When Irving was playing Henry VIII at the Lyceum, a lady was so impressed with the realism of the performance that she offered her baby to replace the property doll used as the baby Princess Elizabeth. The great man replied that there was one small problem: the production probably would run for some time, and since the baby would grow, it might be necessary to provide another at short notice, if she had no objection. And Barry Jackson of the famous Birmingham Rep told the story of an actor who was supposed to burn his hand on a hot stove. He did this so realistically that a lady in the audience was heard to say, "What a thing to leave about on the stage!"

In all these instances we enter the ambiguous world of the theatre. T. S. Eliot believed that human kind could not bear very much reality. In the theatre we seem to choose very little reality and prefer to be involved in the decision making. Thus the playwright often begins, not by asking us to imagine that we are in Verona or Troy, but first by reminding us that we are in a theatre. The conditions of the Elizabethan theatre were such that spectators did not think themselves anywhere else, though, with the Chorus in *Henry V*, they were ready to call upon their "imaginary forces." In one way or another, all drama issues an open invitation to make-believe, and, taking this Chorus as my cue, I will review two or three instances in the drama of the past 400 years to show the phenomenon at its most outrageous.

The Chorus that opens and runs through *Henry V* also ends it, quite artificially with a formal sonnet, so that in fact it provides a kind of frame for the whole play. In one sense, all drama is in a frame that separates the real world from the stage and joins them: the playhouse itself is a frame. But framing a play was a specifically Elizabethan device, one that always called for an unusual degree of license. Inside the frame, the inner play is always at another remove from reality and makes the audience more conscious. The best-known early frame play is *The Taming of the Shrew*, though we are accustomed to seeing it shorn of its frame (and Shakespeare's ending may have been lost), so that it is often reduced to the slight story of Katherine and Petruchio. The subject of the inner play is the marital relationship and "what duty wives do owe unto their husbands," but it is presented as the dream of Christopher Sly, a drunken tinker, which lends a delicious ambiguity to the drama. Like any male chauvinist, he swallows what Kate says about wifely duty, and when he wakes up, promptly demands that the pageboy who has been pretending to be his wife should serve her turn: "Undress you and come now to bed." (Induction, Sc.2.118). He expects her to behave just like Kate, now properly tamed, and "do him ease." He is not to know, poor man, that his beautiful wife is only "a great lubberly boy." We knew it, but then the Elizabethan audience also knew that the actress playing Kate was only a boy as well. So much for the duties a wife may owe her husband.

There is much more to say about the era of boy actresses in England. If any further proof were needed that this was a time of true metadrama, the presence of boys playing girls, with the resultant sex-change games, provides it. When a boy dresses in skirts, the whole masquerade is a species of puppet show, with the audience pulling the strings.

The prime example is *As You Like It*, which sports a boy actor dressed as the girl Rosalind who then pretends to be the boy Ganymede who then pretends to be the girl Rosalind. We should notice that once Rosalind is in doublet and hose, we are constantly reminded of it: she is always complaining. Then the worst happens—her beloved Orlando arrives in the forest, and she hasn't got a thing to wear. When Celia tells her that some ecological vandal has been abusing the young plants by pinning poetry to the trees and carving "Rosalind" on the bark, Rosalind's first response is, "Alas the day, what shall I do with my doublet and hose?" (3.2.215–6).[16] Now any other girl would have slipped quickly back into her skirts, fixed her hair, and made the best of it. Not so our Rosalind. For one thing, the rules say that you cannot change back to your old clothes until act 5. For another, the sex games were about to begin.

First, Rosalind must be chased by another boy actor in the person of Phebe, with revealing results. The more Rosalind tries to shake Phebe off and into the arms of Silvius, the more she clings: "Sweet youth, I pray you chide a year together; / I had rather hear you chide than this man woo." (3.5.64–65). Second, since Orlando cannot recognize her as long as she wears the wrong outfit, she must try to train him a little in the ways of a lover. To do this, the boy actor (R1) turned Rosalind (R2) turned Ganymede (R3) pretends to be Orlando's idea of Rosalind (R4), to the point at which she attempts a mock marriage in which she plays bride, groom, and parson (R5, R6, and R7). Rosalind tells Celia how to be a parson:

> ROSALIND: You must begin, "Will you, Orlando"—
>
> CELIA: Go to. Will you, Orlando, have to wife this Rosalind?
>
> ORLANDO: I will.
>
> ROSALIND: Ay, but when?
>
> ORLANDO: Why now, as fast as she can marry us.
>
> ROSALIND: Then you must say, "I take thee, Rosalind, for wife."

(4.1.116–24)

You may ask why Orlando does not submit to this assault of so many passionate Rosalinds. It is because all he sees is what we see, two young men in doublet and hose holding hands. All he knows is what the Elizabethan audience knows, that they are two young men in doublet and hose holding hands. Orlando may be forgiven for laughing, and we for believing that Rosalind will never get anywhere that way.

It seems impossible for us to re-create, or even imagine, the kind of experience the Elizabethans had when they went to the theatre. In her book *Shakespeare and the Idea of the Play,* Anne Righter suggests that after Hamlet, realism sets in and that thereafter we are well on the way to Ibsen and the gloomy fjords of naturalism. I would demur. Again and again a captive audience proved to be too vulnerable to ignore. If there is an explosion of metatheatre in Shakespeare's comedies, in the sparkling drama of the Restoration the physical circumstances of playing continued to be ideal for playing theatre games and stepping in and out of character. It is quite symptomatic that all Restoration plays are framed by prologue and epilogue, but the exuberant spirit of the drama goes deeper. The Restoration playhouse was among the smallest in history, and its audience tiny by modern standards. I am also among those who still believe that this audience was homogeneous; they knew one another, and going to the play was like throwing a party for your friends. To top this, most of the first actresses were ladies of the evening. A perfect situation for setting up a mountain of Chinese boxes in the name of dramatic make-believe.

The young actresses of the Restoration had a direct contract with the audience that had the extraordinary effect of both framing the play and making their activities in the comedy an extension of their lives. Here is the heroine of Wycherley's *The Gentleman Dancing-Master* on her first entrance:

> To confine a woman just in her rambling age! take away her liberty at the very time she should use it! O barbarous aunt! O unnatural father! to shut up a poor girl at fourteen, and hinder her budding: all things are ripen'd by the sun; to shut up a poor girl at fourteen!
>
> (1.1, p. 131)[17]

Not to be outdone, her maid on the other side of the stage provides the echo: "'Tis true, miss, two poor creatures as we are!" Self-advertisement had never been taken this far before. And in Wycherley's next play, *The Country Wife*, here is Margery Pinchwife with her opening line: "Pray, sister, where are the best fields and woods to walk in in London?" (2.1, p. 265). On the surface, this is the ignorance of a country wife on her first visit to town, but not far beneath the surface the line exchanges an outrageous wink between the gentlemen in the audience and the actress, originally the pert and popular Mrs. Elizabeth Boutel, an implied or real wink that rocks the action of the play.

It may seem that it was only the women of the Restoration stage who could slip in and out of their parts. The leading man could also open and close the gap between himself and his audience. In *The Country Wife*, the hero is one Horner, a rake and a wit, first played by Charles Hart. He is aesthetically ambiguous on several counts. He is out to trick the ladies, but Margery is out to trick him, so that we laugh with and at him. We find him wicked with the same mixture of shock and affection that we might apply to a naughty boy. And this ambivalence is present in his role from the outset, for it is Horner himself who speaks the prologue to the play. He acknowledges that the audience is just as happy backstage as in the pit:

> We set no guards upon our tiring room,
> But when with flying colours there you come,
> We patiently, you see, give up to you
> Our poets, virgins, nay, our matrons, too.
>
> (1.1, p. 249)

His next line is half in and half out of the play, as he introduces the ugly little man who has just entered on the other side: "A quack is as fit for a pimp as a midwife for a bawd; they are still but in their way both helpers of nature." (1.1, p. 249). Another wink to the audience, and with that he steps back into the play proper: "Well, my dear doctor, has thou done what I desired?" (Which was to spread the rumor that he was a eunuch, the better to deceive husbands.) So Horner moves into his play by slow degrees, and before we know it, we have been drawn into his notorious conspiracy.

This period and the eighteenth century were the great age of the aside, that electrifying device that can set a whole theatre by the ears. Insignificant in reading and thus often ignored in literary criticism as a frivolous appendage, it is always of major effect in performance and central to the mechanism of a scene. And the aside has the power to grant that ironic double vision that persuades spectators that they are not only watching the play but also having a hand in creating it. In the best play of the Georgian theatre, Goldsmith's *She Stoops to Conquer*, the asides are brilliant enough to give the impression that the pace of the scenes is faster than it is, that we are watching two plays at work simultaneously without missing a shade of meaning. Recall the first stiff interview between Kate Hardcastle and stuttering lover Marlow:

MARLOW: [. . .] In this age of hyp-hyp-hypocrisy, there are a few who upon strict enquiry do no - a -a - a -
KATE: I understand you perfectly, Sir.
MARLOW: (*Aside*) Egad! and that's more than I do myself!

(Act 2)[18]

They unblinkingly play the game of polite conversation, trotting out one cliché after another. Each is thinking what a hypocrite the other is, ironically underlining the actual subject of this appalling conversation, which is all about—hypocrisy! The result is a parody of every embarrassing exchange between the sexes there has ever been, and we are party to both what they are saying and what they are thinking. The aside defies ultimate analysis.

If the great age of the aside is the eighteenth century, with its smaller theatres, the essential spirit of outer and inner drama continued to flourish vigorously in the popular domestic drama of the nineteenth century. It is enough to cite the curious emergence of the villain of melodrama. He was immediately recognizable by his opera hat, black cloak, thick moustache, and confident swagger. He also had the habit of shaking his fist at the hissing, delighted audience, and if this was not enough he would brandish his legs. In one and the same person he supplied all the basic ingredients of sex and violence. John Hollingshed has left a famous description of one such Victorian villain at work, Bill Sykes in that well-known play *Oliver Twist*. Sykes's big moment came with the death of Nancy:

> Nancy was always dragged round the stage by her hair, and after this effort, Sykes always looked up defiantly at the gallery. . . . He was always answered by one loud and fearful curse, yelled by the whole mass like a Handel Festival Chorus. The curse was answered by Sykes dragging Nancy twice more round the stage, and then, like Ajax, defying the lightning. The simultaneous yell then became louder and more blasphemous. Finally, when Sykes, working up to a well-rehearsed climax, smeared Nancy with red ochre, and taking her by the hair . . . seemed to dash her brains out on the stage, no explosion of dynamite invented by the modern anarchist, no language ever dreamed of in Bedlam, could equal the outburst.[19]

Then, when poor Nancy was no more, Bill would step briskly out of the scene in the traditional manner and take his bow to an equally deafening roar of applause. Was the Victorian audience so childlike that it could laugh and cry, hate and adore, all in one breath?

We would be wrong to think of the twentieth century as the age of realism. It is true that there was a time when the golden rule was, "Thou mayst not break asunder the fourth wall!" When the comedian Hay Petrie was playing Launce in *The Two Gentlemen of Verona* at the Old Vic in 1924, a gentleman in a private box laughed belatedly, and the actor had the temerity to wink at him; it created a small sensation among the critics, and one thought it the most important thing that had happened at the Old Vic during that year. But we may have been deceived by the photographic world of the cinema screen, which by an accident of history coincided with the best of the realistic movement. The truth is that no sooner had *The Wild Duck* and *The Seagull* and other assorted birds flown into view than the great names of the modern theatre wanted to shoot them down. Pirandello, Brecht, Beckett, and Genet have led a long procession of playwrights who demand the earlier freedom of the theatre to swing between the world of the play and the world of the audience. The twentieth century has been marked by a great explosion of creative theatre, and today we are probably more at home with Harold Pinter and Tom

Stoppard, Peter Weiss and Peter Handke, than with Ibsen and Chekhov.

1896 was the year of *The Seagull,* and of *Ubu roi.* Alfred Jarry epitomized self-conscious theatre in his person. A familiar figure in Montmartre, he always carried a pair of loaded pistols, wore old trousers tucked in his socks like a cyclist, went about in a pair of carpet slippers with the toes out, and wore an erect phallus with a little velvet cap (no doubt to spare the feelings of the ladies). The consequence of all this was that it was hard to stay away from his play. The now-familiar setting was aggressively unreal: on the left in a showy wintry scene was painted a large bed with a chamber pot beneath, and on the right were palm trees with a boa constrictor and a gallows from which a skeleton hung. This was no doubt Jarry's idea of a universal (a "global"?) setting. Père Ubu had a pear-shaped head with a huge stomach and a nose like an elephant's trunk, with a bowler hat on top of it all. Nothing wrong with that, you may well think, but when he became King of Poland he carried a toilet brush for a sceptre. Some of the props in *Ubu roi* have now been codified, but is that enough? *Ubu roi* played to a full house made up of Jarry's friends, but even so, the first word of the dialogue (*merdre,* or "shit" with a *r*) produced an uproar that lasted fifteen minutes. Since the same word was repeated no fewer than thirty-five times in the course of the play, the audience went home exhausted (if they got home at all that night).

In 1921 came the play to end all plays, completely collapsing the barriers between the stage and reality. Pirandello's *Six Characters in Search of an Author* was not only a play within a play but also a play without. In the famous Paris production of Georges Pitoëff at the Théâtre des Champs-Elysées in 1923, the actors entered in their everyday clothes through the audience itself, breaking the nineteenth-century rule that actors should know their place. And when they climbed onto the stage, there was nothing on it. Although at this time the surrealist movement was in full swing, nobody had thought of being quite as surrealistic as that. Then when it was the moment for the six Characters to enter, they were lowered to the stage in an old cage lift, a stage elevator previously used for scenery. Paris went wild. The response to seeing six actors lowered in an old stage elevator was, "Look, they're lowering six actors in an old stage elevator." It was a disarming way of saying at the outset that the play was not going to deal in illusion, but simply show how the performance was made; Pirandello was honored by the French government.

The breach with the tradition of illusion was complete, but it was time for complete breaches, and bursting out of the frame served all the more to frame the play everywhere it occurred. Max Reinhardt alarmed the London audience watching his celebrated production of *Oedipus Rex* by having a huge crowd of supers, made up of battalions of drama students and boy scouts, surge through the auditorium of Covent Garden, up the aisles and down a gangway built over the seats. If Greek decorum was conspicuous by its absence, the audience was overwhelmed, and *Punch* carried a delicious drawing of the terrible predicament that awaited any unfortunate spectator who should arrive late only to be swept down the aisle by a forest of Theban spears.

For Pirandello, life itself, like the drama, was illusory. All drama is predicated on a magic "if," and perhaps the imaginative "if" of the theatre and the unpredictable "if" of real life are not that far apart. If Cleopatra's nose had been shorter, Pascal wondered, who knows how it might have changed the course of history? Nor is there any need to return to Cleopatra: Pirandello looked into his own soul and noted in horror that "someone is living my life, and I don't know a thing about him." When the German director Erwin Piscator turned his loudspeakers and his searchlights to his audience, he believed he had turned the theatre into a play-machine, with the playhouse itself "made to dissolve into the shifting, illusory space of the imagination."[20]

All this is heady stuff, because in the last analysis there is no barrier between the actor and audience, and a good performance will always complete the imaginative circuit of the theatre, the electricity flowing between the stage and the spectator and back again. Quince's problems about how to prove that the lion was only Snug the joiner, and how to bring moonlight into the playhouse when the sun was shining, were fundamental, and yet no problem at all. Pirandello and his trick of projecting the modern consciousness as a piece of theatre, Brecht and his elaborate devices to involve an audience by the paradox of alienation, Genet and his cynical symbolist games of mock ritual and role-playing, all were manipulating reality, as any good drama must, so that the audience could see with fresh eyes. Good theatre implies that, as we sit together in the audience, I'm in your play and you're in mine, which all goes to prove that convention, if convention be admitted, has no certain limitation.

NOTES

1. Patrice Pavis, *Languages of the Stage* (New York: Performing Arts, 1982), 146.

2. J. L. Styan, *Shakespeare's Stagecraft* (Cambridge: Cambridge University Press, 1967), 199.

3. Norman Rabkin, *Shakespeare and the Problem of Meaning* (Chicago: University of Chicago Press, 1981), 27.

4. Wilfried Passow, "The Analysis of Theatrical Performance," *Poetics Today* 2, no. 3 (1981): 238.

5. Pavis, *Languages of the Stage,* 111.

6. Keir Elam, *The Semiotics of Theatre and Drama* (London and New York: Methuen, 1980), 43.

7. Dryden, John, "Of Heroic Plays: An Essay" in *Dryden,* ed. George Saintsbury, Hill and Wang, New York, n.d., p. 11.

8. Johnson, Samuel, "Preface to Shakespeare" in *Johnson on Shakespeare,* ed. Walter Raleigh, Oxford University Press, London, 1908, pp. 26–28.

9. Edward Braun, trans., *Meyerhold on Theatre* (London: Methuen, 1969), 53, 62.

10. Wallace Fowlie, *Dionysus in Paris* (New York: Meridian Books, 1960), 21–31.

11. Tyrone Guthrie, *A Life in the Theatre* (New York and Toronto: McGraw-Hill, 1959), 350.

12. Ibid.

13. Anne Righter, *Shakespeare and the Idea of the Play* (London: Chatto and Windus, 1962), 20.

14. Passow, "The Analysis of Theatrical Performance," 237.

15. *The Arden Shakespeare.* Subsequent quotations will be taken from this edition.

16. Lionel Abel, *Metatheatre: A New View of Dramatic Form* (New York: Hill and Wang, 1963), 57–8.

17. W. C. Ward, ed., *William Wycherly* (London: Ernest Benn, 1949). Subsequent quotations will be taken from this edition.

18. Oliver Goldsmith, *She Stoops to Conquer,* in *Collected Works of Oliver Goldsmith* [Ed. Arthur Friedman] (Oxford: Clarendon Press, 1966), Vol. 5, p. 147.

19. Erroll Sherson, *London's Lost Theatres of the Nineteenth Century* (London: John Lane, 1925), 38.

20. Erwin Piscator, *The Political Theatre,* trans. Hugh Rorrison (New York: Avon Books, 1978).

Self-Referring Artifacts

ANNA WHITESIDE

The premise of this essay is, as Anne Ubersfeld and Keir Elam have suggested,[1] that a theatrical sign is both a sign and a referent, a hyphenated sign-referent: at once a sign of something and the thing or things referred to by the actors. Thus, the concrete theatrical referent seen onstage refers, in turn, to itself as a mimetic theatrical sign. This may sound tautological until we remember that a referent is both a concrete thing or state of affairs[2] and that to which one refers, whatever its ontological status. The first is the logician's referent, the second that of speech-act theorists and philosophers of language.

Since this essay deals primarily with a particular aspect of theatrical reference, a preliminary definition may be useful. By reference I mean (1) the relationship that obtains between an expression and what it stands for on a particular occasion, namely, its reference (this is Lyons's definition)[3] and (2) the process and thus the act of referring to the referent (Donnellan, Searle, and Strawson in particular stress this view).[4] My aim here is to show some of the ways in which theatrical reference is primarily self-reference, something manmade, an artifact. Since this is particularly obvious in modern theatre (as in modern fiction and poetry), my corpus will be limited to twentieth-century theatre. Broadly speaking, the examples will fall into three categories: (1) scenic objects and décor, (2) characters, and (3) acts or action (including speech considered as speech act). All three categories of self-referring artifacts refer not just to themselves but, obviously, to theatre as theatre.

Self-reference is the occupational hazard of all involved with theatre. It concerns all artistic creation and re-creation and is the inevitable correlate of our awareness of the poetic function. Even "historical" theatre, which supposedly refers to "real" events, refers to them as History with a capital H, which is none other than a particular, approved version: a story, consecrated by time and thus fixed in a seemingly immutable scenario. The very fact that history is retold (just how many versions of Joan of Arc are there besides Shaw's, Anouilh's, and Bresson's?) shows that films and theatre merely imitate historians by reinterpreting so-called historical facts. Like history, which, with the passage of time, comes to refer to itself as his story or her story—that is, as ideological history in the Althusserian sense—so theatre too refers to itself as theatre: as both imitation and invention.

Before launching into examples of self-reference, let us first return to the sign-referent. In Ionesco's *Jacques ou la soumission,* the horse to which Roberte II and Jacques so excitedly refer in their joint storytelling suddenly rushes across the stage—not as a horse, but as a flaming mane. Ah yes, we say, synecdoche, a partial sign referring to the equine whole. Better still, we may construe it as another type of metonymy: the literal image of what their burning passion has ignited, or more ironically, the dashing mane as the only perceptible element of a horse moving so fast that the eye perceives no legs, no body.

How should these two impassioned storytellers have eyes for more? They are preoccupied with each other and they with their joint creative and procreative storytelling enterprise. They are caught up in a frenzy of ardor: "Dépêchons-nous . . . dépêchons-nous," they cry, just as the ardent artifact, born of their mutually enflaming storytelling, appears from the wings and sails across the stage.[5]

This flaming mane is both sign and referent. It is there on stage, albeit briefly, and is referred to by both Jacques and Roberte. Yet at the same time, it is they who, in their storytelling, have created it, so that at last it can rush across the stage. Thus, this strange hybrid sign-referent is in fact a referentially created artifact born of the very story it illustrates, one as strange as the other. As an artifact, then, it refers to itself as artifice, a dramatic deformation of both horse and mane, and so to theatre as creation, as illusion, as illusion that fools no one.

Similarly, the English clock in *La Cantatrice chauve* and its seventeen English strokes, referred to by Monsieur Smith, who remarks "Tiens, il est neuf heures," are signs that this is not "reality," but theatre. As Jean Giraudoux's actress Raymone remarks, playing herself in *L'Impromptu de Paris:* "Si la pendule sonne 102 heures ça commence à être du théâtre," especially if, as here, a character has just reminded us that, in so-called realist theatre, when one said that it was five o'clock, a clock used to strike five.[6]

Conversely, theatrical sign-referents may draw attention to themselves as artifacts by being more "real" than the pseudoreality they are meant to evoke. The portrait of Jacques' grandfather in Ionesco's *L'Avenir est dans les oeufs* begins to make encouraging gestures to Jacques, who is about to lay the eggs of posterity. The large picture frame does, indeed, contain the grandfather's portrait, or rather an actor representing it, as well as "Grand-père Jacques" himself, portraying himself in the flesh: both sign and referent. Even when he walks out of his picture frame, he is still a sign-referent and, as such, refers to the other characters as sign-referents, too, by his interaction with them.[7]

A similar portrayal occurs in Ionesco's "guignolade," *Le Tableau*, with the difference that here the picture appears first, hung proudly on the wall by its rich owner, "le gros monsieur." It is then re-created by him, as he fires his pistol at his decrepit old sister, Alice, whose visible signs of ugliness (arm stub, filthy disheveled old wig) are instantly and miraculously transformed to reveal a young and beautiful Alice, now identical to the portrait. But, at the same time, this rejuvenated Alice is turned into a statue of the portrait; "Je suis artiste," cries the gros monsieur, "J'ai créé un chef d'oeuvre. . . . J'ai surpassé le modèle! J'ai fait mieux que le peintre."[8] But though superior, in that the likeness is now three-dimensional, his statuesque chef-d'oeuvre is as artificial as the portrait it refers to; it is no longer Alice, but stands for her. In fact, it is an ironic reminder of the life his creation has just taken, as the neighbor who pops in just after the pistol shot, seeing Alice transformed, remarks: "Tiens, vous achetez des statues . . . Et un tableau aussi? On dirait que le tableau est une copie de la statue."[9] And so, all sign-referents (picture, statue, and character) refer to one another and, in the process, to theatrical creation as fleeting re-creation of something that lives only to die again, once the re-creation is over. In much the same way, the whole of Ionesco's play *Le Roi se meurt* refers constantly to the inevitable mortality of a king who must die with his role, at the fall of the curtain: "Tu vas mourir dans une heure et demie," says Marguerite, his first wife. "Tu vas mourir, à la fin du spectacle."[10]

In a sense, the whole question of whether theatre is the real thing or not rests with the spectator, as Stoppard's ambiguous play, *The Real Thing*, suggests. But from the performance point of view, there is often a concerted effort to show that to oppose reality and theatre is to create a false dichotomy. Perhaps it is the impromptu, as a meta-theatrical subgenre, which brings this out most clearly. From Molière to Ionesco, via Pirandello, Giraudoux, and Cocteau, all the elements of theatre are presented as equivocal self-referring artifacts.[11] As in countless other plays within plays, these authors refer to themselves as both author and character, creator and created. For example, Ionesco appears as a character in his *L'Impromptu de l'Alma;* he is both the playwright inventing and trying to write the play as well as the character on the stage playing the writer. When asked by the three critics, Bartholomeus I, Bartholomeus II, and Bartholomeus III, all carbon copies of one another, to read his play, he simply rereads the opening stage directions and lines of this Ionesco impromptu we are watching I, II, and III times. At the same time that Ionesco creates himself as writer-character—and here he is the only real character in the double sense of the word, the critics being dummies (in every sense)—he creates his play, and, by performing it, theatre. By the same token, he makes his faceless critics self-referential artifacts, since these learned doctors reproduce, almost verbatim, actual theatre critics' reviews, previously published in *Théâtre populaire,* in the case of Bartholomeus I and II, and in *Le Figaro,* in the case of Bartholomeus III. The three critics' implicit self-indictment further diminishes their theatrical credibility and thus exposes the falseness of their godlike status as judges. Their shadow roles are shown to be the mere ritual of pseudoreligion, an impression that becomes even clearer when, chased offstage by Marie, the down-to-earth maid, they mutter in the wings unseen, as one voice: "Costumologie, costumitude, théâtrologie, psycho-spectatologie . . . tologie . . . tologie . . . tologie . . ."[12]

Pedants are popular with Cocteau, too. His amusing *Impromptu du Palais-Royal* is constantly interrupted by the *spectatrice,* who starts off by correcting the actors' pronunciation before the "play" even begins. The first actor to appear slips onstage in front of the curtain, while putting on his costume as *Premier marquis:* "Je n'aimerais pas être la dupe de cet imbroglio," he confides to the audience, referring to the play that is about to begin. "Imbreuio," corrects the spectator, explaining that: "On ne prononce pas le prince de Broglie mais le prince de Breuil. Imbroglio se doit prononcer imbreuio." By her intervention, she refers to herself as an actor, too, a pseudospectator who neverthe-less represents the token spectator: "Il est vrai," she says, "que je suis de la maison. Seulement j'assiste à ce spectacle en spectatrice et je profite d'une latitude que l'auteur nous laisse pour interrompre le jeu et faire en quelque sorte la salle y tenir son rôle."[13]

This latitude is just as illusory as the so-called impromptu, since, as the players remark, every word is written down. And yet at the same time as the imbroglio is being fabricated before our eyes in a false improvisation, it is there as genuine performance, as performance referring to performance alias illusion on the one hand, and performance as reality on the other. The illusion constitutes the framework. As the play opens, the actor who plays the marquis slips onstage, still dressing for the play before the curtain rises; he shows himself as actor about to become character. At the end, as the curtain falls and rises for the curtain calls, again we see the actors as actors, this time in various stages of dress and undress, as they prepare for their next roles, or dress to return home.

As in Genet's theatre, this reference to illusion as illusion also refers to the actor as an actor in real life: one adept at creating illusion. Again, as in Genet, we realize that role-playing is a reality. For Genet it is both a theatrical and a social reality. Theatrical, since we see the inmates of *Le Balcon* and their clients actually dress up on stage (in the brothel) as executioner, thief, judge. Each of these petty characters playing bishop, judge, and general is purposely made to seem theatrical, "plus grand que nature . . . par un acteur qui montera sur des patins de tragédien d'environ 0,50 m de haut"[14] and by each character's exaggeratedly magnificent costume. Conversely, the powerful financier is shown downgrading himself as he dons an unkempt wig over immaculately groomed hair to complete the illusion of a man "vêtu en clochard."[15] Similarly, in *Les Nègres*, blacks are made to seem like blacks pretending to be white;[16] in Peter Shaffer's *Equus*, horse masks are to be made in such a way that they reveal the human heads behind them.[17] Role-playing is shown as a social reality corroborated by, and thus mirroring, society: Genet's judges, generals, bishops, governers, queens, thieves, maids, grand ladies, and gentlemen are the puppets of our social fiction: a publicly condoned, and economically sustained, role-playing, shown on stage as precisely that.

For Cocteau, role-playing, and theatre in general, refer to a more purely aesthetic reality. In fact, Cocteau sets out to demonstrate in his *Impromptu du Palais-Royal* that reality and theatre are one, since theatre, by fusing illusion and reality, becomes its own reality. The food on stage, being mere cardboard, is here referred to as such, luckily for the king, Louis XIV, or rather the actor playing him, who confesses to the guest Molière that he could never eat as much as Louis XIV used to, since he has to watch his weight. While the pseudo-Molière and the pseudo-king sit at table, the actor playing the duke fumes at having to play a subservient role and wait on this Monsieur Molière so far beneath his rank; in fact all the actors are quite scandalized by this breach of etiquette. Here, characters and actors are no longer mutually exclusive categories; they refer to one another sometimes as actors, sometimes as characters, and in so doing refer to themselves as the actor-characters they are and thus to themselves as illusion in the making. We are told that Molière was never really a guest at Louis XIV's table; similarly, what we are seeing on stage is a scene that refers to history as invention/illusion. To make the point, on comes the Duc de Saint-Simon, or rather on he rolls, since he has had his ear glued to the keyhole and so loses his balance when the king flings open the door. Here, then, is Saint-Simon on stage, creating "history," noting Cocteau's maxims, calling them Molière's, and creating his story of the legendary meal, at which Molière was Louis XIV's guest—a meal legendary in the full sense of the word, since in fact it never took place but exists as legend. This dramatic creation is a real creation: the cardboard food is actually there and referred to as real cardboard; the legendary meal is being created as a legend, invented before our very eyes. Louis XIV's celebrated phrase, "J'ai failli attendre," which he never said, is now said by the king, as he makes the paling actor-duke "taste" the suspicious-looking soup he's about to serve: "M'obligerez-vous à répéter une de mes phrases les plus fameuses?" asks the king.[18] The poor duke tastes and totters, though he only pretended to taste—such is the power of theatrical persuasion. Contaminated by his own role, he believes he is poisoned.

Quotes and false quotes abound in Cocteau's *Impromptu,* as do re-created versus fictitious characters and events. Their very coexistence is mutually undermining and enhancing. Both are shown on the same level, neither being privileged, for, like any quote, a change of context brings about a change of reference, creates an original pseudoquote. The quote, like dialogue, is made unique by each performance: no single reiteration is more or less real than another. "Notre métier," says Cocteau's character Molière, "consiste à confondre le vrai et le faux."[19] As though to prove the point, he then chides the smart alec stage manager for announcing him as Monsieur Poquelin: "Je vous prie de m'annoncer sous le faux nom que j'ai rendu véritable,"[20] and so the stage manager reannounces Cocteau's Molière, playing a pseudo-Molière, who never lived this scene as "Monsieur Molière," erstwhile *homme de théâtre.*

Cocteau's invented Molière playing a pseudo-Molière is, nevertheless, self-referential; the role itself refers to Molière the actor, who played so many of his own roles, and the writer, who realized so much of his own fiction on the stage. In Cocteau's *Impromptu,* for example, switching briefly to a scene from *Le Misanthrope,* Molière plays Alceste (as he did in the past) opposite the serving duke, who, with obvious relief, jumps out of demeaning servitude into Oronte's role, quoting the latter's reply to Alceste. This soppy, lovelorn reply in a play within a play quotes, distorts, and thereby ridicules an even earlier sonnet that Molière wrote as an amorous youth. This sonnet, which Cocteau makes Oronte (alias the duke) recite uninterrupted a few minutes later as the youthful declaration of love it originally was, and not as Oronte's foolish, foppish, verbal mincing, is seen as quite different, "fort beau" in fact, now that its change of context, and thus of performance style, has transformed it back into an expression of youthful ardor.[21] Here is a theatrical demonstration that performance, and thus context, both immediate and implied, is all: this double performance refers to the creative as well as re-creative function of theatre, to the implied double context of any theatrical performance. Performance, then, is essential to reference, as Oronte's sonnet parody shows. It constitutes an act in both senses—an act and consequently an act of self-reference; performance as performance; a self-referring artifact, remade with each performance.

Since the other obvious examples (Pirandello's *Six Characters in Search of an Author* and *Each in His Own Way,* and, less significantly, Giraudoux's *L'Impromptu de Paris*) also explore questions similar to the ones we have just examined, I would like to move on from self-referring performance and creation (verbal and otherwise) to the process of reference itself as something created before us on stage. Jean Tardieu's *Un mot pour un autre* provides an amusing example of apparently referential nonsense. After Tardieu gives us a décor which is "plus 1900 que nature" (i.e., referentially overdetermined and thus décor as décor), his two main characters, Madame and Madame la comtesse de Perleminouze, proceed to converse in what appears to be completely nonreferential discourse. In the following extract, the

maid announces to Madame the visit of Madame's bosom friend, Madame la comtesse de Perleminouze. "Ah," replies Madame, "Quelle
grappe! Faites-la vite grossir!" Madame then greets the countess:

Retour de la Bonne, suivie de Madame de Perleminouze

LA BONNE [*annonçant*]: Madame la comtesse de Perleminouze!

MADAME [*fermant le piano et allant au-devant de son amie*]: Chère, très chère
peluche! Depuis combien de trous, depuis combien de galets n'avais-je
pas eu le mitron de vous sucrer!

MADAME DE PERLEMINOUZE [*tres affectée*]: Hélas! Chère! j'étais moi-mème
très, très vitreuse! Mes trois plus jeunes tourteaux ont eu la citronnade,
l'un après l'autre. Pendant tout le début du corsaire, je n'ai fait que
nicher des moulins, courir chez le ludion ou chez le tabouret, j'ai passé
des puits à surveiller leur carbure, à leur donner des pinces et des mous-
sons. Bref, je n'ai pas eu une minette à moi.

MADAME: Pauvre chère! Et moi qui ne me grattais de rien![22]

Despite all appearances, we easily discern in this play a standard
drawing-room comedy plot. Madame is having an affair with the
count, and, because he foolishly appears while his wife is visiting, the
countess discovers all. In fact, the plot refers to itself as a stereotype
in the making, just as the dialogue refers to itself as cliché, as phatic
function and pure process of communication. We do not need to
know what is being said; the situation, gestures, and prosody refer us
to a stock situation that we know by heart before it begins. All we have
to do is recognize the familiar, as in the following example; after the
game is up and the count withdraws discreetly, Madame la comtesse
de Perleminouze says, after a pregnant silence:

MADAME [*désignant la table à thé*]: Mais, chère amie, nous allions tortiller!
Tenez, voici justement Irma! *Irma entre et pose le plateau sur la table. Les
deux femmes s'installent de chaque côté.*

MADAME [*servant le thé*]: Un peu de footing?

MADAME DE PERLEMINOUZE [*souriante et aimable, comme si rien ne s'était
passé*]: Vol-au-vent!

MADAME: Deux doigts de potence?

MADAME DE PERLEMINOUZE: Je vous en mouche!

MADAME [*offrant du sucre*]: Un ou deux marteaux?

MADAME DE PERLEMINOUZE: Un seul, s'il vous plaît!

(pp. 217–18).

and the curtain falls!

In much the same way, Cocteau's *Parade*, with no dialogue at all, refers to itself, not so much as an act of communication, although it is one, but as a parade in the making, a spectacle, an aesthetic transposition into different modes of creation: mime, dance, music, and art, each mode referring to its own and the others' mutually creative powers of stylized interpretation.

Now, if interpretation is creation, it follows that theatre is self-creating and, as such, refers to itself autotelically, as an act and process of becoming.[23] This is obviously true of the *Impromptus*, but is also true, for example, of a film like Alain Robbe-Grillet and Alain Resnais's *L'Année dernière à Marienbad*. We watch the creative process referring to itself mimetically as the elusive liaison between the man and the woman gradually acquires substance through being referred to over and over again, each time within an increasingly substantial context. As we watch fiction becoming more and more substantial, we see it transforming itself into reality.

Marguerite Duras's *Hiroshima mon amour* shows a similar creation of reference by destroying, paradoxically, even the uniquely referring function of the proper name (for many philosophers, proper names are the only true referring expressions) and by subordinating Hiroshima's original historical reference, even to some extent its topical reference, when the French actress designates her Japanese lover as Hiroshima, "Hiroshima, mon amour," her lover and also her love, love that refers to universal love, symbolized by this anonymous couple.[24]

In Apollinaire's *Les Mamelles de Tirésias*, Thérèse's breasts refer to her femininity; they are her "appas féminins." As Thérèse changes gender and flounces out of her feminine role to become Tirésias, however, these signs referring to femininity detach themselves from her and float up and away in the form of two balloons. Now they refer to themselves as theatrical props, as self-referring artifacts in the very process of self-reference, floating between androgyny and their own autonomy. As if this were not enough, Thérèse, becoming Tirésias, also retrieves from the same feminine hiding place balls with which she proceeds to pelt the audience, to drive the message home; reference, albeit self-reference, relies on communication between performers and spectators.

The self-referential process of communication in *Les Mamelles* was given special prominence in a recent Texas production. Spectators beheld not only a pair of artificial breasts converted into balloons but

Anna Whiteside

also pairs of painted breasts emblazoned on every T-shirt of the mixed male and female chorus standing on stage; they beheld one set of referents referring to another and both sets referring to themselves as artifacts, and thus to theatre itself as representation of the act of self-reference.

NOTES

1. Anne Ubersfeld, *Lire le théâtre* (Paris: Editions Sociales, 1977), 32–3; Keir Elam, *The Semiotics of Theatre and Drama* (London and New York: Methuen, 1980), 30.

2. For C. K. Ogden and I. A. Richards in *The Meaning of Meaning* (London: Routledge and Kegan Paul, 1923), the referent is something that is an actual thing or state of affairs. For Bertrand Russell, in "On Denoting," *Mind* XIV (1905): 479–93, it is above all related to the question of truth and existence. Charles S. Peirce is considerably more flexible, since he sees the referent, or sinsign in his terminology, as something that both exists and acts as a sign: "an actual existence thing or event which is a sign."

3. John Lyons, "Reference, Sense and Denotation," *Semantics,* vol. 1 (Cambridge: Cambridge University Press, 1977), 174.

4. This is implicit in Keith Donnellan, "Reference and Definite Descriptions," *Philosophical Review* LXXV (1966): 282–304; John Searle, "The Logical Status of Fictional Discourse," *New Literary History* 6, no. 2, (1975): 319–32; Leonard Linsky, "Reference and Referents," *Referring* (London: Routledge and Kegan Paul, 1967), 116–31.

5. *Théâtre I* (Paris: Gallimard, 1954), 123.

6. Jean Giraudoux, *L'impromptu de Paris, Théâtre III.* (Paris: Grasset, 1959), 168.

7. Eugène Ionesco, *Théâtre II* (Paris: Gallimard, 1958), 219.

8. Eugène Ionesco, *Théâtre III* (Paris: Gallimard, 1966), 270.

9. *Théâtre III,* 271.

10. Paris: Gallimard (Folio), 1963, 37.

11. "Theatre" as distinct from "drama," according to Elam's distinction in *The Semiotics of Theatre and Drama:*

Theatre is taken to refer here to the complex of phenomena associated with the performer-audience transaction: that is, with the production and communication of meaning in the performance itself and with the systems underlying it. By 'drama', on the other hand, is meant that mode of fiction designed for stage representation and constructed according to particular ('dramatic') conventions. The epithet 'theatrical', then, is limited to what takes place between and among performers and spectators, while the epithet 'dramatic' indicates the network of factors relating to the represented fiction [2].

12. *Théâtre*, 2: 5.

13. Paris: Gallimard, 1962, 17.

14. Paris: Gallimard (Folio), 1979, 19.

15. Ibid., 52–3.

16. "LA COUR.—Chaque acteur en sera un Noir masqué dont le masque est un visage de Blanc posé de telle façon qu'on voie une large bande noire autour, et même les cheveux crépus." *Les Nègres*, (Paris: L'Arbalète, 1958), 16.

17. Harmondsworth, Middlesex and New York: Penguin Books, 1973, 15: "On [the actors'] heads are tough masks made of alternating bands of silver wire and leather; their eyes are outlined by leather blinkers. The actors' own heads are seen beneath them: no attempt should be made to conceal them."

18. Paris: Gallimard, 1962, 35.

19. Ibid., 27.

20. Ibid., 27–8.

21. Presumably, Cocteau is also referring indirectly to the fact that elsewhere in *Le Misanthrope*, Molière quotes (and deforms) Dom Garcie de Navarre; in the original, the words are tragicomic, whereas in *Le Misanthrope* they are more tragic—not to mention the fact that Eliante's words originally were spoken by a man in the *Dom Garcie* version:

DOM ALVAR: Qu'avez-vous vu, Seigneur, qui vous puisse émouvoir?
DOM GARCIE: J'ai vu ce que mon âme a peine à concevoir;
    Et le renversement de toute la nature
    Ne m'étonnerait pas comme cette aventure.
    C'en est fait . . . Le destin . . . Je ne saurois parler.
DOM ALVAR: Seigneur, que votre esprit tâche à se rappeler. . . .
DOM GARCIE: Ah! tout est ruiné;
    Je suis, je suis trahi, je suis assassiné. . . .
        (*Dom Garcie, IV*, 7, in Molière, *Oeuvres Complètes* I
        [Paris: Gallimard, 1971], 385)

ELIANTE: Qu'est-ce donc? Qu'avez-vous qui vous puisse émouvoir?
ALCESTE: J'ai ce que sans mourir je ne puis concevoir;
    Et le déchaînement de toute la nature
    Ne m'accablerait pas comme cette aventure. C'en est fait . . .
    Mon amour . . . Je ne saurais parler.
ELIANTE: Que votre esprit un peu tâche à se rappeler.
ALCESTE: Ah! tout est ruiné;
    Je suis, je suis trahi, je suis assassiné. . . .
        (*Le Misanthrope*, 4.2. Molière, *Oeuvres Complètes II*, 194.)

22. Paris: Gallimard, 1966, 210–211.

23. For a fuller discussion of autotelic reference see W. Krysinski, "Poland

of Nowhere, the Breasts of Tiræsias and Other Incongruities," in *On Referring in Literature,* eds. Anna Whiteside and Michael Issacharoff (Bloomington: Indiana University Press, 1987).

24.   ELLE: Hi-ro-shi-ma, C'est ton nom. . . .

LUI: . . . Ton nom à toi est Nevers. Ne-vers-en-Fran-ce.

Paris: Gallimard (Folio), 1960, 124. In fact, this retrospective naming, at the very end of the film, is superfluous since we already identify them as Lui and Elle. The topological naming identity merely underlines their universality, rather than indicating their specific identity.

Much Ado About Doing Things With Words (and Other Means): Some Problems in the Pragmatics of Theatre and Drama

KEIR ELAM

Shakespeare is an all too convenient textual and cultural peg for discourses dramatical, dramaturgical, or dramatological, and this essay (though born in a sense of a direct encounter with Shakespearean comedy[1]) takes the play abused in the title in precisely this opportunistic fashion—that is, as a handy point of departure and return for some remarks of a more general and theoretical nature. Shakespeare abused, however, has a way of avenging and defending himself through the unwitting ironies he inflicts on the abuser, and here what the titular reference might suggest is an admission that the very subject of the essay, doing things with words (and other means), is really equivalent to "Nothing" and that talking *about* doing things with words, as I intend to do, is just so much idle ado—which may well turn out to be the case: "Notes, notes, forsooth, and nothing."

But one might also reverse this suggestion and claim on the contrary that the Much Ado of Shakespeare's comedy is not really about Nothing at all but is precisely about various things done with words and other means (but especially with words). And indeed what the comedy itself repeatedly supposes, despite its title, is that words may do very powerful and consequential and in fact dangerous things: Beatrice's words, for example, cut Benedick to pieces, or so he says; their friends' words provoke love between Beatrice and Benedick, or so it is suggested; Don John's words shock Claudio out of his love for Hero, or so he claims, and other words persuade him back into love again; and Claudio's words in turn kill Hero, or so he and others are led to believe. Now all of these verbal deeds do, it is true, involve inventions or fabrications or fictions; hence Shakespeare's "Nothing." Yet this is in a sense the very nothing of dramatic representation itself, which is similarly founded on inventions, fabrications, and fictions. What I wish to do here is to consider or reconsider some of the ways in which the dramatic representation can be approached precisely as an effective and consequential and even dangerous *doing things* about, or by means of, the fictional *doings* it shows forth—and some of the very dangers inherent in talking *about* such *doings*.

This is the territory of what is fashionably termed pragmatics, specifically in this case the pragmatics of theatre and drama or of dramatic theatre. Charles Morris, in his extremely influential tripartite division of semiotics (into syntactics, semantics, and pragmatics), defines pragmatics as "that portion of semiotic[s] which deals with the origin, uses, and effects of signs within the behavior in which they occur."[2] It would be possible to write a history of semiotics and linguistics, or more generally of what were once called the sciences of language (including literary studies), in terms of the paradigmatic shifts over Morris's three "portions" or branches. If formalist and structuralist models of language and other sign systems privileged syntax, then the concern with codes and the production of meaning that succeeded it (roughly in the 1970s) had an obvious semantic basis or bias. At present, beyond question, the governing paradigm is pragmatic. Code has been largely replaced by context, and meaning-production by meaningful interaction, as the dominant objects of recent linguistic and semiotic inquiry.

The corpus of theories and models that are often grouped under the general rubric of pragmatics ranges from discourse analysis, conversation analysis, and text linguistics (broadly concerned with linguistic and other signs in use) to modal logic, the theory of possible worlds, cognitive sociology, and frame analysis (dealing primarily with users and their epistemic operations) to ethnomethodology, interactional sociology, and the aesthetics of reception (concerned, roughly, with contexts and effects). But there is no doubt that the most widely and frequently invoked analytic framework, the true Prince of Pragma, is the so-called theory of speech acts proposed by J. L. Austin and developed by John Searle and countless others.[3] The

winning advantage the speech-act theory offers in accounting for
semiotic interaction, or at least linguistic interaction, is that it unites
all of Morris's pragmatic factors—uses, users, and effects—in a single
and hermetically sealed system. Thus the use of language (specifically, the illocutionary act) necessarily presupposes the intentions of
its user (the illocutionary force of the utterance) and is not complete
until received and understood as such by the listener (illocutionary
effect or "uptake," together with other kinds of effect, which I will
return to later). This is a far neater, and, as the Chomskyans used to
say, far more powerful model of meaningful interaction than that offered by any of the alternative theories. Partly because of this explan-
atory power and economy and partly because speaking is generally
accepted as the exemplary mode of symbolic action, speech-act theory
has inevitably come to be widely applied to nonlinguistic or secondary
symbolic systems: to the visual arts, to literature (provoking not always helpful questions like "What kind of speech act is a poem?"),[4]
and not least to theatre and drama. The onetime hegemony of the
old "linguistic model" in semiotics has become the hegemony of the
speech-act model, and especially the illocutionary model. So that
what I want to say here will be essentially limited to the testing of
speech-act solutions for some of the knottier or naughtier problems
of theatrical and dramatic communication. These are the dangers
that I mentioned. And my observations will be—let me make my own
illocutionary intentions clear straightaway—more of an ideological
and historiographical than of a specifically semiological nature.

In a sense the drama seems to offer itself as an ideal happy hunting
ground for semiotic exploration *sub specie pragmaticae.* Etymology
alone suggests as much. Drama, as any decent introductory manual
on the subject will begin by saying, derives from the Greek *dran,* "to
do." And pragmatics derives likewise from Greek, from *pragma,* "act,"
which in turn comes from the verb *prattein,* again "to do." What more
natural object for the science of doing than the art of doing? And if
one glances back over the history of Western thinking about drama
and theatre, one rapidly discovers that dramatic theorists have always
been acutely aware of the eminently pragmatic nature of their object.
Aristotle, as everyone knows, defined the dramatic representation as
an imitation of "people engaged in action, doing things."[5] Julius Caesar Scaliger, neoclassical legislator in matters poetical, decreed that
the dramatist's task is "teaching through action;"[6] Dryden claimed
that the dramatic author should subordinate everything to the rep-

resentation of action;[7] and Pirandello, in a celebrated slogan that is remarkably close to the terms of Austin, Searle, and company, designates dramatic dialogue as "spoken action."[8]

Pirandello is making explicit here what is in effect implicit throughout this history of reflection on the art of doing—namely that the main kind of action in the Western dramatic tradition has been spoken doing. In Aristotelian terms, it is mainly *lexis* that carries forward the narrative *praxis*. It is on these grounds, naturally, that the drama irresistibly invites the application of (in Searle's terms) "a theory of language [as] part of a theory of action."[9] Indeed, I don't think it is too fanciful to claim that speech-act theory itself is founded on a dramatic model of language use. *Totus mundus loquitur ut histrionem:* "All the world's a dialogue." In other words, the speaker-speech act-listener dialectic outlined by Austin is, not only in its component but also in the *purity* of the symbolic action it proposes—a purity that corresponds only notionally to the rough and ready and often directionless *praxis* of our everyday speech exchanges—close to the interactional intensity of dramatic dialogue. The drama distills and institutionalizes the social and interpersonal force of discourse, shaping the desultory and uncertain action of natural conversation into a dynamic chain of events, or if you like into a plot. In this sense, Professor Austin works better with Mr. Shakespeare and Mr. Shaw than with, say, Mr. Smith and Mr. Brown and their ordinary conversational doings. Hence Richard Ohmann's discovery that the drama "rides on a train of illocutions,"[10] a discovery remade by numerous commentators in recent years.[11]

There is no doubt that illocutionary analysis does work in providing a moment-by-moment of doing-by-doing breakdown of the dialogic ation, and thereby permits us to overcome once and for all the unhelpful literary critical dichotomy between *lexis* and *praxis*, or between "diction" and plot. This in itself is a considerable critical conquest. And in a broader perspective, illocutionary typologies may well help identify the global proairetic patterns of the drama and its language and so act as authentically hermeneutic and not merely heuristic tools. In the case of Shakespeare's *Much Ado*, for example, the dominant illocutionary event is what Searle in his typology of illocutionary acts classifies as the "representative," that is, the type of speech act that commits the speaker to the truth of his or her utterance (e.g., affirmations, denials, accusations).[12] And in fact the comedy might be seen as a dramatization of the problems relating to such truth-bound acts and to the "essential" and "sincerity" conditions that render these acts "happy" or "unhappy." The absence of these conditions, and with them the lack of commitment to the truth of the utterance, is another important aspect of the "Nothing" of Shakespeare's title.

But there is, it seems to me, a real danger in this approach, the first of the dangers involved in talking about dramatic doings. This is the danger of "illocutionizing," as it were, the entire verbal structure of the drama. The risk is that of a reductively positivistic or even Benthamite conception of verbal doings: if not a Gradgrindian "facts! facts!" then at least a Searlean "acts! acts!" In rhetorically rich and multiform dramas—Shakespearean comedy being an exemplary case in point—what is done with, and still more what is done to, words goes far beyond the simple performing of codified social deeds such as accusing or commanding or offering. Take, for instance, the flytings or insult matches between Benedick and Beatrice that everyone remembers in *Much Ado*. What counts in these exchanges is not their illocutionary status, since they are made up more or less of a series of affirmations, but the kind of rhetorical virtuosity on show, the inventiveness of the insult varying itself. Or take the farcical scenes involving Dogberry and his malapropisms in the same play, in which it is the lexical and semantic structure of the abused mother tongue that provides the main business, albeit comic business. These are modes of verbal doing—rather than forms of decorative diction—that have little to do with the speech act proper. There are more things done with dramatic discourse than are dreamt of in your philosophy, John Searle.

This branch of doing things with words has to do with the internal axis of the drama,[13] or with the fictional communication between the dramatis personae. But dramatic and theatrical interaction is not, of course, limited to the fictional domain, and the illocutionary model has also been applied to the external axes of the drama—that is, to the relationships between the fictional exchange itself and the real communicational contexts within which the dramatic text is composed or represented or received. The first of these relationships is the one arising between dramatist and text, and so involves the intentionality or force of the text itself as communicative act. There is again a lengthy historical pedigree to the notion that the dramatic text and its very composition represent modes of symbolic doing. Here another etymological feat or feast is called upon. Philip Sidney for example following Scaliger, observes that the word *poet*—by which

Scaliger at least means dramatic poet—"cometh of this word *poeiein,* which is 'to make': wherein," he adds proudly, "I know not whether by luck or wisdom, we Englishmen have met with the Greeks in calling him a maker." [14] Now making, as Sidney is anxious to demonstrate, is a purposeful kind of acting or doing, and indeed in a didactic conception of theatre such as Sidney's or Scaliger's, the primary communicative act is precisely the dramatist's doing to or doing toward the audience. Dramatic composition becomes, as it were, a making of doings—that is, a delegating of the primary (external) communication to the secondary (internal) interaction, which, as Sidney insists, encodes it ("things not affirmatively but allegorically and figuratively written"). [15] Teaching *through* action, as Scaliger puts it.

A strikingly analogous view of the dramatic text as a set of fictional acts encoding the playwright's "serious" or nonfictional communicative intentions is offered by Searle himself in his reflections on the logic of fiction—with the difference that the immediate addressees of the playwright's serious illocutions are not the spectators but the actors. "The text of the play," argues Searle, "will consist of some pseudo-assertions, but it will for the most part consist of a series of serious directions to the actors as to how they are to pretend to make assertions and to perform other actions"; and he continues: "the author of the play [unlike, say, the novelist] is not in general pretending to make assertions, he is giving directions as to how to enact a pretense which the actors then follow." [16] The text thus becomes a kind of global or macro-illocution of the type that Searle classifies as the "directive"—that is, an attempt to get the receiver, in this case the actors, to do something, in this case to act his play in the way he indicates.

Here is another danger; this conception of the semiotic status of dramatic composition, which curiously enough is shared by certain semioticians of theatre who wish to *deny* the primacy of the text, [17] seems to me descriptively banal and historically blinkered, not to say substantially wrong. What it entails—and Searle is perfectly explicit about this—is the apotheosis of the authorial stage direction, or as it were the stage directive, as the real communicational substance of the text. The dialogue, by the same token, is relegated to the margins as an "unserious" if not unnecessary extra, the mere let's-pretend kid's stuff at which otherwise all-too-serious adults agree somewhat irrationally to play. Significantly, Searle gives as his *exemplum* of a text made up "for the most part" of directions or directives John Galsworthy's *The Silver Box,* a play in which, in effect, the author sends interminable messages to directors and actors (whom he obviously does not trust to do their jobs): "*Act I, Scene i. The curtain rises on the Barthwick's dining room, large, modern, and well furnished; the window curtains drawn. Electric light is burning . . .*"—everything down to the make of the butler's cotton socks. But this form of dictatorial or deontic delirium, far from being the historical norm, is merely the expression of a very particular type and particular period of unilateral *literary* theatre in which the dramatist elects himself as director, stage manager, lighting operator, and tea lady. What are we to make, in this perspective, not only of *Oedipus Rex* but even, to return to our Shakespearean touchstone, of *Much Ado*, whose directional interventions, at least in the Quarto and Folio texts, are limited to *exeunt* and *manent*. Very unserious, or again an ado that would amount, for Searle, almost to nothing. But even in the case of the most writerly of writers' theatre, as with the plays not only of Galsworthy but also of Shaw and Maugham and others, the chances are that the dramatist's "serious" acts will remain unfulfilled or, as the jargon has it, unhappy. Which is to say that any director worth a directorial chair will tend to take the author's directions—if you will excuse the lexical pileup—not as directive but as so much pseudonarrative information that can be used or discarded according to need. What remains is precisely the fictional doing, or dialogue.

The second "external" relationship that has been treated in illocutionary terms regards the *praxis* or practice of the actor with respect to the fictional acts he or she utters. Austin's passing comment to the effect that a speech act will be "in a peculiar way hollow if said by an actor on stage"[18] has since been taken up and elaborated into a kind of revised standard version of dramatic representation according to which what the act performs is the mere locutionary act of uttering, in Austin's rather inelegant terms, the "vocables" and "noises" (i.e., words and other units) of the text, while the illocutionary act proper is attributed to the dramatic speaker.[19] There is no question that this principle of the actor's limited liability for the represented deeds, verbal and otherwise, is logically and ontologically, not to say juridically, impeccable. If this were not so, Olivier would be in jail for murdering and remurdering Gielgud. Only the English Puritans failed to make such an elementary distinction. But as such, this tells us nothing, and perhaps less than nothing, about the role of the actor in performing those acts for which he or she is not legally responsible. To elect the performer as the transparent "locutionary" vehicle for the pragmatic material of the drama is, at the very least, an idealistic canceling of the actor's very real stage presence, or stage practice, and *its* materiality. In no school of acting, whether, say, Stanislavski's with its ideal of bridging the psychological and experiential divide between the actor's saying and character's doing, or Brecht's, which instead drives a strategic wedge between the two, but only in order to expose the actor's material mediation, would so legalistic a notion of actorial commitment be taken seriously.

And what if we were to reverse the priorities of this supposed actor-text rapport, so that the represented dramatic exchange becomes on the contrary the "locutionary" vehicle for the actor and his or her only too opaque presence. Obvious cases come to mind. When Elizabeth Taylor "appears in," as they say, *The Little Foxes,* the real semiotic force of the performance becomes not so much to represent as to *present* the actress herself in a suitable and convenient role. Not to mention those more serious historical theatrical traditions, such as the *Comédie-Française* or the English actor's theatre from Garrick to Kemble, the main aesthetic force of which comes precisely from the institutionalizing of this histrionic priority. Actors may be more than empty vessels waiting to contain the dramatist's fine illocutionary wine.

The final conquest of what we might call, not altogether unfairly, the illocutionary imperialism of recent years has been the external orientation proper of the performance—that is, the transaction between stage and audience. Morris, you will remember, mentions as one of the chief concerns of pragmatics the "effects" of signs, and it is obvious that no semiotic model of communication can do without a theory of reception. There is little doubt also that the accounts of audience response furnished to date by semiotics or by sociology or by the aesthetics of reception have been anything but convincing in the case of the theatre. So it is not surprising if certain theorists have turned for help or inspiration in this matter to speech-act theory and its version of effects. Ross Chambers, for example, has proposed that the theatrical performance as an overall communicative act encodes, rather like the text for Searle, a macro-illocution of the "directive" variety, namely an offer or invitation to the audience, paraphrasable in the performative phrase "I offer myself for interpretation," or perhaps "I invite you to interpret me."[20] The performance or performers, then, send out a kind of polite visiting card to the spectators bearing the message "come and interpret me."

There are two main risks in this kind of operation. One is the general and obvious risk of trying to squeeze into the illocutionary holdall more than it is capable of containing. The performative paraphrase game that Chambers applies to the performance is easy to play and can be adapted to any event in any form of behavior. Still, in theatrical terms, when the curtain goes up we might have the encoded performative "We invite you to stop chatting to your neighbor and to pay attention"; a set change becomes the declaration "We are now in another place"; the interval is translated into the directive "Buy your ice cream and visit the restroom now"; and so on. This is simply another symptom of the dominance in contemporary semiotics of the speech-act metaphor, which, as I said earlier, has effectively taken over from the linguistic model of the distant 1970s. Where once we searched for minimal units and double articulations in every corner, we are now busy hunting out performative phrases. In practice, the visiting card sent out by Chambers's performative performance is no more nor less than the founding convention of the theatrical transaction itself: the spectator knows as part of his elementary theatrical competence that he is called upon to interpret what he hears and sees. So that if each performance does no more than renew this statutory invitation, then the overall act it performs is at best tautological, not to say feeble.

The second risk is more serious, and here I arrive at the ideological considerations I promised or threatened earlier. There is a brilliant passage in Sidney's *Apology* on this very question of effects, in which he argues for the moral superiority of dramatic and other poetry over philosophy on the grounds (with a glance at Aristotle) that the "practical" efficacy of poetry is greater: "it is not *gnosis* but *praxis* that must be the fruit."[21] Which means that the stage-audience interaction is not primarily a matter of cognitive processing (*gnosis*) but a matter of direct persuasive action toward the spectator (*praxis*). Or as Austin would put it, the dramatic representation, unlike philosophical discourse, is not constative but directly performative (the poet "nothing affirms," adds Sidney). In the illocutionary version of audience reception suggested by Chambers and others,[22] it is on the contrary *gnosis* and not *praxis* that must be the fruit. Or in other words, a spectator whose role is limited to that of a more or less passive decoding by invitation only is involved in a very pallid mode of *praxis* indeed.

This, it seems to me, is one of the central ironies in contemporary semiotic inquiry: that is, the the more "pragmatic" it becomes, the less it has to do with actual *pragma*. There is much talk in contemporary literary and theatrical semiotics of the "work" of the reader or spectator as the most important element in the communicational process, but more often than not, the labors assigned to the reader or spectator are such cerebral tasks as inferring or hypothesizing or presupposing or, of course, understanding and interpreting the acts performed for his or her benefit. And so while the "receiver" is undoubtedly the favorite object at present of the semiotic model-building club, he or she is generally speaking a somewhat disembodied and spectral receiver, a kind of ghost in the machine, to abuse Arthur Koestler's phrase: an ideal extension of the epistemic and logical operations of the text, be it narrative text or performance text. So that what passes for pragmatics, especially in the theatrical field, is in danger of being a sort of phenomenology of robotism.

Some light is thrown on this problem, as on most semiological problems, by Roland Barthes. In his book *La chambre claire*, Barthes, reflecting on the effects that photographs have upon him, makes a distinction that is, I think, equally suggestive for theatrical reception.[23] One kind of response Barthes terms the *studium*, "the application to something, the taste for something, a sort of alert, but not particularly intense being interested."[24] This cool interest Barthes contrasts with what he calls the *punctum*, an irresistible pricking or injury: "This time, I am not the one who goes in search of him . . . but it is he who, setting out from the scene [*la scène*, which one might also translate as 'stage'] goes through me like an arrow."[25] The terms of Barthes's definition of the *punctum*, of that mode of painful and compulsive pleasure that is not sought out but actively seeks out and injures the receiver, are remarkably close to those of Sidney's rhapsody on the superior pleasure of dramatic and other narrative poetry. The philosopher, says Sidney—and here we are in the territory of pure *studium*—"showeth you the way, he informeth you"; the poet on the contrary "with a tale forsooth . . . cometh *unto* you, with a tale which holdeth children from play and old men from the chimney corner."[26] This is the *punctum:* he cometh unto you; you do not, as Barthes says, go in search of him.

Sidney's vision of the dramatist's Orphic powers over the auditors goes back, of course, to Aristotle's *Poetics* and its theory of *pathos*. *Pathos:* suffering, the injury, the *punctum*. This is the presiding deity of the *Poetics* as it is of *La chambre claire*. Barthes revisits the *Poetics* in founding his own poetics of photographic reception. Without the punctum or pathos, he argues, there is no compulsion, no passion, no motivation in the encounter with the image—and so no authentic interaction or *praxis*. The philosopher showeth you the way, informeth you, but by the arts we want to be sought out, held irresistibly from the chimney corner.

The problem with much of what goes under the name of theatrical pragmatics (or theatrical semiotics in general) is that it is strictly and, one might say, strategically limited to the temperate zone of the *studium* and keeps a safe distance from the tropics or dangers of the *punctum*. The "illocutionary" level of interaction—with the purely cognitive decoding it entails—together with the related mental toils of presupposing, inferring, hypothesizing, and the rest, remains safely and comfortably within the bounds of Barthes's "alert but not particularly intense" application to the object. Of course, we as students or theorists of theatre, including theatrical reception, necessarily operate within the terms of the *studium*, a professional "application to" or "being interested in." But does this mean that we must attribute an analogous cool studiousness to our model spectator, or to ourselves as actual spectators? Is the semiotics of theatrical communication, in other words, destined inescapably to be a *studium* of the *studium* alone, or is it not possible to conceive instead of a semiotic conception of the *punctum*, or *pathos*, or if you like audience passion, that compulsion which, as Sidney and Barthes tell us, motivates the receiver's active participation in the artistic practice?

It is, naturally, more than possible to conceive of a theatrical transaction absolutely devoid of *pathos* in any form. Indeed, passionate or passional response to the performance is probably, and unhappily, a rare enough experience for all of us, as it is for Barthes and his few irresistible photographs. And there have been didactic theories of dramatic representation that programmatically *exclude* passionate audience response in favor of a cooler, more contained, and more cognitive mode of reception: Horace's,[27] for example, or Scaliger's, or more recently Brecht's. Brecht's expulsion of *pathos* is one of the founding moves in his rejection of Aristotelian "dramatic theatre" in favor of a didactic epic theatre. The dramatic theatre, says Brecht in one of his most famous essays, "implicates the spectator in a stage situation"; it "provides him with sensations"; the spectator "shares the experience," is "involved in something." Epic theatre, on the contrary, "turns the spectator into an observer"; the spectator is "brought to the point of recognition"; he "stands outside, studies."[28] The spectator studies: *studium*, the theatre "is no longer the place where his interest is aroused but where he brings it to be satisfied."[29] I seek him out, he cometh not unto me. Brecht's model auditor is strategically restrained from trespassing beyond the bounds of an alert but not too intense decoding, a controlled coming-to-consciousness of the encoded message. But this limitation is less a scientist or intellectualistic bias on Brecht's part than a precise ideological choice, a *postponement* of the real passion and of the real praxis to the extra-theatrical sphere of revolutionary social action.

The expulsion of *pathos* within contemporary semiotic inquiry, and especially within speech-act theory, is also an ideological choice, but in this case a choice of a rationalistic or idealistic nature. In Austin's original speech-act typology there is indeed a very clear and precise equivalent to the Aristotelian *pathos*—namely what he baptizes the "perlocutionary effect." "Saying something," he observes, "will often, or even normally, produce certain consequential effects upon the feelings, thoughts, or actions of the audience . . . and it may be done," he adds, "with the design, intention or purpose of producing them."[30] We may, for example, persuade or move or delight or amuse or alarm our listeners. In some ways, this intentional and consequential doing things to the audience, the perlocutionary act, is the most complete kind of speech act in Austin's system, the truly interpersonal and social praxis to which the locution and illocution lead. And it is, as he says, a normal aspect of our communicative doings. And yet later philosophers of language and linguists and semioticians have all but disowned the perlocutionary effect as an unphilosophical embarrassment or extrasemiotic contamination. Too dangerous. Perlocutionary acts, as someone once said, should be prohibited in public. This is clearest in the case of Searle himself, whose *Speech Acts* barely mentions perlocutions at all, and who restricts his discussion of consequences to the illocutionary effect, the simple understanding of the act. What people do with words, it would seem, is to express and receive propositional contents and illocutionary forces.

It is interesting to see how the consequences of this exclusion emerge particularly clearly—or one might say dramatically—in Searle's treatment of theatrical reception. At the end of his illocutionary analysis of the representation, he asks, somewhat riskily, "Why bother?" and explains, "That is, why do we attach such importance and effort to texts [or performances] which contain largely pretended speech acts?"[31] Searle's embarrassed "Why bother?," his bemusement at all the ado about pretended doings, is surely provoked by the very attempt to explain audience interest and audience motivation in terms of illocutionary effect, as if the performance were a kind of ontological party game or philosophical charade. Why we bother may have to do with our hope that the performance will work other effects on us than getting us to understand—that is, that it will persuade or move or delight or amuse or even, maybe, alarm us. An invited and *desired* danger.

Which is to say that a "pragmatic" semiology of theatre, and especially of dramatic theatre, is bound to espouse some notion of perlocutionary or persemiotic effect if it does not wish to take as its object of inquiry a sort of playgoer's tea party, all courtesy and mutual comprehension. This is also, in a sense, a historical necessity. All of the major theories, both descriptive and prescriptive, of theatrical representation, from Aristotle to Artaud, have been powerfully teleological: they are based on the end product, on the very possibility or ideal of an emotional, moral, or practical punch packed by the performance. Theatre has always been, or has always been thought to be, an essentially perlocutionary enterprise, its end and its motivation lying in persuasion or delight or purgation or instruction. What vary, with historical circumstances and ideological principles, are the precise perlocutionary objectives and of course the means of achieving them. I would like to dedicate the last part of this essay to a brief overview of some of the most important historical perlocutionary models of dramatic representation as a first and very rough indication of what such models involve.

In Table 1, the various elements of the representation are arranged vertically. The main division is between the first four elements (2 to 5), which have to do with the internal axis of the drama, the represented interaction (hence the horizontal arrows), and the last five elements (7 to 11), which concern instead the external axis, or interaction between performers and audience. Category 6, the epistemic rules governing the representation, is a kind of middle ground between the two. The perlocutionary package as such is represented here, naturally, by the last two elements (10 and 11). In this respect, there is an immediate distinction to be made that is, I think, of some interest, if only historical. This is Austin's own distinction between the perlocutionary object (10), or the effect of the communication on the audience, and the perlocutionary sequel (11), the practical consequences of the act. Some models—Aristotle's, Castelvetro's, Coleridge's—are purely object-ended, which is to say that the transaction

Table 1. Some "perlocutionary" models of dramatic representation

	Aristotle	Horace	Scaliger	Castel-Vetro
1. Type of model	Pathetic-purgational	Didactic	Oratorical-didactic	Hedonistic
2. Mode of representation ↔	Imitation (of events)	Imitation and narration	Imitation and narration	Imitation of subject from history
3. Type of representation ↔	Pitiful and fearful deeds	Common deeds clothed in dignity	Actions as signs of dispositions	Rare (pitiful and fearful) deeds
4. Dominant element of drama ↔	Plot (*mythos*)	Recognizable character types	Exemplary characters and their attitudes	Plot ("morals are accessories")
5. Conventional constraints on action ↔	*Hamartia;* recognition; peripety; unity of action	Unnacceptable acts narrated, not shown; no *deus ex machina;* appropriateness and consistency of acts	No absolute criteria; "action is the only essential"	Unities of time, place and action; acts similar to, but not identical with, historical deeds
6. Epistemic rules of representation ↕ ↔	Necessity or probability of acts	Verisimilitude of agents and acts	Representation of truth	Possibility that events might have happened
7. Role of actor ↑ ↓	Vehicle for poetry; not essential to tragic effect	Vehicle for poetry	Vehicle for poetry	Vehicle for poetry
8. Performance constraints ↑ ↓	Visual elements subsidiary; gesture should be restrained	Only 3 actors; chorus as actor; performance for select audience	—	—
9. Audience attitude ↑	Recognition; identification	Recognition of types; identification with good	Acceptance of truth of representation	Recognition of own good in hating injustice becomes "oblique pleasure"
10. Perlocutionary object	Pity and fear become delight, leading to purgation of pity and fear	Instruction; knowledge (persuasion)	Desire to embrace good (N.B., not purgation)	Purgation of emotion
11. Perlocutionary (post-theatrical) sequel →	—	Melioration of society	Social harmony	—

52

Table 1. (*continued*)

	Sidney	Coleridge	Fuchs	Artaud	Brecht
1	Didactic-moral	Phenomenological	Passional-mystical	Passional-anarchic	Didactic-revolutionary
2	Iconic imitation (speaking picture)	Imitation of men acting (narrative in representation)	Ritual enactment	Ritual enactment; collective ceremony	Imitation as narration
3	Heightened (heroic) deeds	Pathetic or amusing actions	Actions as death/rebirth rites	"Cruel" interaction	Actions as indicators of social *gestus*
4	Notable images of virtues and vices	Emotional experience of agents	Passion (emotional, religious) of agents	Unrepresentable necessity of life (in its "cruel" intensity)	Attitudes of agents toward actions
5	The unities: beginning in *medias res;* decorum	According to genre	Absolute nudity of expression	De-psychologized "metaphysics" of verbal and gestural acts	Underlining of events; nonlinear development; exposure of *gestus*
6	Does not affirm; shows truth allegorically; creates a "golden" world	Imitation of reality under a semblance of reality (dramatic illusion)	Stage as microcosm of world—the space of redemption	Not illusion but "dangerous reality"	No illusion; no "magic"; not representation but "showing"
7	Vehicle for poetry	Actor as vehicle for poet's idea; no excessive advertising of own presence	Actor as pure passion, as vehicle of the divine	Sacrifice of personality to "vital sincerity"; trance state	No transformation; no identification; *gestus* of showing
8	Dignified presentation; no vulgar clowning for easy laughter	Intimate space (the stage as near as possible a "closet")	Abolition of distance between performer and audience; no divison between stage and auditorium	Performance as system of "hieroglyphic" signs; no hierarchy; acting as sacred rite	Exposure of all elements; materiality; no trance; acting with taut muscles
9	Identification with good	Temporary and voluntary half-faith; half-waking state; projection of emotion and sensation onto agent	Perfect communion with actors in passion rites	Experience of suffering object	Brings interest to be satisfied; studies; takes up critical position with regard to action
10	Instruction and delight lead to desire to practice	Delight from balance of feelings and thoughts leads to emotional satisfaction	Experience of spiritual death/rebirth	Unbearable pain leads to contagion by "plague"	Knowledge and pleasure from critical awareness of social causes
11	Melioration of society	—	Reunion with God	Return of society to original chaos	Revolutionary praxis

is exhausted in the emotional, spiritual, and intellectual experience in the theatre itself. Castelvetro is explicit about this when he declares that the theatrical experience produces "no profit" (not at the box office but after the show).[32] These are purgational or hedonistic or phenomenological models, more descriptive than prescriptive. The others are all sequel-ended, founded on the ideal of a direct influence on posttheatrical social practice, whereby the perlocutionary object itself, the theatrical response proper, becomes merely instrumental. These are didactic or religious or revolutionary models of theatrical praxis, more prescriptive than descriptive. In classical moral theories—Horace's or Scaliger's or Sidney's—the postdramatic sequel is the direct melioration of civilization by means of instruction in the good, instruction that leads to a more tightly welded social harmony. This tradition is violently and strategically reversed, of course, by Artaud, for whom the performance should have the effect of disintegrating artificial social bonds through the unbearable individual suffering experienced by the spectator, thereby throwing society back into original chaos, from which it might be reborn.[33]

What interests me particularly in these models is the relationship between the kinds of effect aimed at and the modes of representation that supposedly produce them, or, if you like, between the bottom half and the top half of the table. It is this dialectical rapport that should be the main concern of a pragmatics of dramatic theatre. It is immediately apparent that the classical models from Aristotle to Sidney (and well beyond) are strictly dramaturgical. The role of the actor and of performance conditions is ignored or denied. Aristotle claims that the actor's physical mediation is not even essential to *pathos*, which derives exclusively from the represented action, and this is more or less the established tradition for centuries. The reverse is true, of course, of expressionistic and post-Artaudian theory and practice, in which the represented dramatic action is reduced in importance or all but eliminated, and the only *praxis* that counts is the direct interaction between actors and audience. An extreme case in point is the mystical expressionism of Georg Fuchs,[34] for whom the theatrical experience is a direct collective participation in a death and rebirth rite, abolishing the internal/external divide and leading to the triumphant sequel of a complete spiritual reunion with God.

But the one constant feature of these models and their inner logic is the symmetry or direct specularity between the internal and external interaction. Both Scaliger and Brecht, for example, whose models—Scaliger's of an oratorical-didactic and Brecht's of a didactic-revolutionary character—are strikingly analogous in several respects, elect the internal interaction primarily as a means of exposing the attitudes or dispositions behind the actions (Brecht's *gestus;*[35] see element 3). This entails a more diegetic or narrational conception than a mimetic conception of action (element 2). In Brecht, this exposure is mirrored in the actor's *gestus* of showing the action and the attitudes of his character (element 7). And in both cases it induces in the spectator a particular ideological stance toward the action and what it demonstrates (element 9): an acceptance of its truth in Scaliger and a critical awareness of the exposed social gestus in Brecht. Hence in each case there is a bringing-to-consciousness with regard to social *praxis,* an effect that mirrors the dramaturgic exposure of the agents' attitudes.

In the object-ended models, on the contrary—Aristotle's, Castelvetro's, Coleridge's—the represented interaction is not ethically instrumental but aesthetically autonomous. Castelvetro is again bluntly candid here: "Morals are accessories," he declares. And so the mode of representation is purely mimetic. Here the mirroring lies in the fact that the perlocutionary or pathetic effect of the representation itself corresponds necessarily to the perlocutionary or pathetic consequences of the internal dramatic action (element 3). Aristotle's pity-and-fear–provoking deeds have just this double internal/external efficacy. This mirroring in turn necessarily entails an audience attitude (element 4) of identification or projection, precisely what the Brechtian model excludes.

There are some very suggestive, if scattered, remarks by Coleridge on the phenomenology of audience projection in the experiencing of effects. Coleridge sets out—and this is surely the right pragmatic emphasis—from the active roles of the audience, beginning with the collective act itself of gathering together in the theatre, which he defines as a place of "amusement thro' the ear or eye in which men assemble *in order to be amused* by some entertainment presented to all at the same time."[36] And this spectator initiative is present in the process of identification, in which he projects "a sort of temporary half-faith, which the spectator encourages in himself and supports by a voluntary contribution on his own part, because he knows that it is at all times in his power to see the thing as it really is."[37] The spectator, in other words, willingly delegates his or her own *praxis* and emotional experience to the represented action because of the perlocutionary returns the spectator expects to receive, so that even the experience of the *punctum* is an active suffering projected onto the internal doings: "The mind . . . attributes the painful sensation received to a corresponding agent."[38] Hence the internal/external mirroring process.

There is no time to examine the table in greater detail here: I leave it to the reader to decipher as a posttextual or, optimistically, as a perlocutionary sequel. But these considerations do in a way bring us back, just to conclude, to Shakespearean comedy. Because while *Much Ado* obviously does not pretend to the pathetic density or intensity of the tragedies, it is indeed concerned above all with the effects of reception, the act of listening or overhearing, or much ado about nothing, as the punning title would have it. And the effects it dramatizes are eminently and dangerously perlocutionary in a kind of internal or introjected model of the intended external effects: "What fire is in mine ears?" "She died upon his words." "She speaks poniards, and every word stabs." Every word stabs: this is the injury, the *punctum*, the danger without which audience reception or noting would be but a disinterested note-taking. Too little for so much ado.

NOTES

1. This essay was written during the preparation of the author's volume *Shakespeare's Universe of Discourse: Language-Games in the Comedies* (Cambridge: Cambridge University Press, 1984).

2. Charles Morris, *Signs, Language and Behavior* (Englewood Cliffs, N.J.: Prentice Hall, 1946).

3. J. L. Austin, *How to Do Things with Words,* 2nd ed. (London: Oxford University Press, 1976); John Searle, *Speech Acts* (Cambridge: Cambridge University Press, 1969).

4. See Samuel R. Levin, "Concerning What Kind of Speech Act a Poem Is," in *Pragmatics of Language and Literature,* ed. Teun A. Van Dijk (Amsterdam: North Holland, 1976), 141–60.

5. Aristotle, *Poetics,* trans. Gerald F. Else (Ann Arbor: University of Michigan Press, 1967), 19.

6. Julius Caesar Scaliger, *Poetics* (1561), trans. F. M. Padelford, in *Critical Theory since Plato,* ed. Hazard Adams (New York: Harcourt Brace Jovanovich, 1971), 137–43.

7. John Dryden, *Of Dramatic Poesy: An Essay* (1668), ed. George Watson (London: Dent, 1962).

8. Luigi Pirandello, "Spoken Action," in *The Theory of the Modern Stage*, ed. Eric Bentley (Harmondsworth: Penguin, 1968), 153–57.

9. John Searle, *Speech Acts: An Essay in the Philosophy of Language*. Cambridge: Cambridge University Press, 1969, p. 17.

10. Richard Ohmann, "Literature as Act," in *Approaches to Poetics*, ed. Seymour Chatman (New York: Columbia University Press, 1973), 81–107.

11. See, for example, Alessandro Serpieri, "Ipotesi teorica di segmentazione del testo teatrale," in *Come comunica il teatro: dal testo alla scena* (Milan: Il Formichiere, 1978), 11–54; Keir Elam, *The Semiotics of Theatre and Drama* (London: Methuen, 1980), 156–70; Jeannette Laillou Savona, "Narration et actes de parole dans le texte dramatique," *Etudes littéraires* 13, no. 3 (1980): 471–94; Ross Chambers, "Le masque et le miroir: Vers une théorie relationnelle du théâtre," *Etudes littéraires* 13, no. 3 (1980): 397–412; M. H. Short, "Discourse Analysis and the Analysis of Drama," *Applied Linguistics* 11, no. 2 (1981): 181–202.

12. John Searle, "A Taxonomy of Illocutionary Acts," in K. Gunderson, ed., *Language, Mind and Knowledge* (Minneapolis: University of Minnesota Press, 1975), 344–69.

13. This terminology is borrowed from William Dodd, "Metalanguage and Character in Drama," *Lingua e stile* 14, no. 1 (1979): 135–50.

14. Philip Sidney, *An Apology for Poetry* (1595), ed. Geoffrey Shepherd (London: Nelson, 1965), 99.

15. Sidney, *An Apology*, 124.

16. John Searle, "The Logical Status of Fictional Discourse," *New Literary History* 6 (1975): 319–32.

17. See Anne Ubersfeld, *Lire le théâtre* (Paris: Editions Sociales, 1977), 255–58; Marco De Marinis, *Semiotica del teatro: L'analisi dello spettacolo* (Milan: Bompiani, 1982), 48–59.

18. Austin, *How to Do Things with Words*, 22.

19. See, for example, R. M. Gale, "The Fictive Uses of Language," *Philosophy* 46 (1971): 324–40; James O. Urmson, "Dramatic Representation," *Philosophical Quarterly* 22 (1972): 333–43.

20. Chambers, "Le masque et le miroir," 403.

21. Sidney, *An Apology*, 112.

22. See also De Marinis, *Semiotica del teatro*, 170–73.

23. Franco Ruffini invoked Barthes's distinction (round-table discussion on the semiotics of theatre, Centro di Semiotica Teatrale, Prato, Italy, January 14, 1983) as grounds for the abandoning of the semiotic enterprise altogether, especially in its application to theatre—a conclusion or consequence that is perhaps unduly drastic.

24. Roland Barthes, *La chambre claire* (Paris: Editions du Seuil/Gallimard, 1980), 48.

25. Ibid., 48–9.

26. Sidney, *An Apology,* 113.

27. Horace, *Art of Poetry,* trans. E. C. Wickham, *Critical Theory,* ed. Hazard Adams, 69–75.

28. Bertolt Brecht, *Brecht on Theatre,* ed. John Willett (London: Methuen, 1964), 37.

29. Ibid., 55.

30. Austin, *How to Do Things with Words,* 101.

31. Searle, "The Logical Status of Fictional Discourse," 332.

32. Lodovico Castelvetro, *The Poetics of Aristotle Translated and Explained* (1570), trans. R. L. Montgomery, in *Critical Theory,* ed. Hazard Adams, 145–53.

33. Antonin Artaud, *The Theatre and its Double,* trans. Mary Caroline Richards (New York: Grove Press, 1958).

34. Georg Fuchs, *Die Schaubühne der Zukunft* (Berlin: Schuster & Loeff, 1905); *Die Revolution des Theatres* (Munich: Müller, 1909); *Die Sezession in der dramatischen Kunst und as Volksfestspiel* (Munich: Müller, 1911).

35. Brecht, *Brecht on Theatre,* 198–201.

36. Samuel Taylor Coleridge, "Desultory Remarks on the Stage, and the Present State of the Higher Drama" (c. 1808), in *Shakespearean Criticism,* vol. 1, ed. T. M. Raysor (London: Dent, 1960), 176–83.

37. Ibid., 178.

38. Ibid., 179.

Stage Codes

MICHAEL ISSACHAROFF

Code is a loaded word. It can, of course, mean a collection of laws or rules applying to a specific situation: this is its legal meaning. But it can also mean a system for communication, as in Morse code, in which "arbitrarily chosen words, letters or symbols are assigned definite meanings."[1] The confusion arising from the use of the term stems at least in part from its two distinct (though related) meanings.

In literary theory, and particularly in semiotics, the term *code* has been one of the single richest sources of confusion, simply because it denotes so many different types of systems. It is often misused, widely misunderstood, sometimes meaningless. For Roman Jakobson, in his famous "Closing Statement," it is a sign system "fully, or at least partially common to the addresser and addressee."[2] The metalingual function, it will be remembered, is the instance of language focusing upon itself for the purpose of verifying the code (i.e., lexical use) in a given speech event. Significantly, listening to Jakobson's paper at the Indiana University conference on style in language in 1958, René Wellek pointed out in his closing remarks that code "might better be called 'convention' or 'tradition' in literature."[3] Even if reservations may be expressed about other aspects of Jakobson's system of the six functions of language,[4] his use of the word *code* is clear: it denotes a specific language, *in toto*, as a communication system.

I do not propose to use the term *code* as Roland Barthes did in *S/Z*, with its odd quintuped beast: hermeneutic, semic, symbolic, proairetic, and cultural. As Barthes himself admits, these codes cannot always be clearly differentiated. Although his analyses of segments of Balzac's story are suggestive, if not brilliant, his method is far from rigorous and his concept of code never clearly defined, except insofar as we are told that it is a "mirage de structures." "Le code," he writes, "est le sillon de ce déjà."[5] The problem is that Barthes's *déjà* is arbitrary and will almost certainly vary considerably from competent reader to competent reader. Barthes defines the déjà as the "Livre" (de la culture, de la vie, de la vie comme culture)—a series, as he puts it, of "voices off"—a picturesque, though rather hazy, concept.

If we were to expect greater precision on this issue from Michael Riffaterre, we should be disappointed. In *Semiotics of Poetry*[6] or in his more recent *La Production du texte*,[7] the word *code* is used to denote a variety of related verbal phenomena of differing length and complexity, including "conventional discourse" and "technical discourse" (e.g., heraldic discourse)—which is not unreasonable—but it also stands for the "symbolic use of language," "idiolectic usage," as well as for virtually any word or words centering on a given theme or activity in which the word or words are not to be taken at face value, that is, where we can detect a key to hidden meaning. This enables the author of *Semiotics of Poetry* to speak of a garden code, a street scene code, a floral code, a sunlight code, an animal code, a whole poem that is a code for another, a metaphoric code, and so forth. If there are as many codes as words, in a specific text or corpus of texts, the usefulness of the concept is jeopardized. However, Riffaterre's use of the term is far clearer when it denotes "discursive convention," as in his very suggestive earlier work dealing with clichés and similar forms of verbal convention. Jonathan Culler shares the view that the literary semiotician's task is to examine conventions, and in his *The Pursuit of Signs,* makes the following programmatic statement:

> Just as the task of the linguist is not to tell us what individual sentences mean but to explain according to what rules their elements combine and contrast to produce the meanings sentences have for speakers of a language, so the semiotician attempts to discover the nature of the codes which make literary communication possible.[8]

Implicit in the same critic's definition of a code as a "set of objects or categories drawn from a single area of experience and related to one another in ways that make them useful logical tools for expressing other relations"[9] is another criterion relevant to our present concern: a code must contain more than one signal! (The signals are also limited in number.)

Finally, in this matter of codes, the point should be made that it would be inappropriate to expect the codes of a literary (or dramatic) text, if one talks of codes at all, to resemble logical or technical codes. The latter, such as Braille, semaphore, Morse, the highway code, and, of course, the alphabet, are rigorous, unambiguous systems whose signs are fixed and conventionalized. Literary texts, including plays, do contain some such codes, such as language, and comparable systems (e.g., proxemic, kinesic, and cultural). But the literary text is not usually a mere passive repository for codes such as these. It may contain conventionalized codes with which an author feels at liberty to tamper (this is one of the phenomena that Riffaterre examines to great effect). It may also create its own conventions and thus its own codes. In a way, then, this brings us back to Barthes's idea of each literary text as its own model. Herein therefore lies the paradox of the theatre semiotician's enterprise: the playscript is a mix of codes conventional and codes unpredictable.

One final word to conclude these introductory remarks. If one decides to retain "code" as an operational concept, it is clear, I think, that Keir Elam's broad distinction between theatrical codes (those specific to the individual performance) and dramatic codes (those relating to conventions generic, structural, and stylistic) will be useful.[41] To those broad categories I shall add a third: stage codes (and hence my title)—specific to the individual playscript. Inevitably, though, an individual script may contain codes belonging to the other two categories, as well as codes that are not intrinsically theatrical or dramatic.

● ● ●

One of the fundamental problems central to research in the semiotics (even in the theory) of drama is the way in which the various codes and systems of signs that make up a performance or a script are wedded to form a coherent whole. The resulting scheme of interlocking systems is to some extent determined, if not explicitly prescribed, by the playscript itself. My main concern here will be the playscript and, specifically, the manner in which systemic focus is inscribed in the text. We shall find, of course, that very often the verbal channel is crucial. Both the didascalia and the dialogue act as constraints on the virtual or on the ultimate performance.

That a performance is a complex polysystem of signs and codes is self-evident. However, segmentation of the performance, or even of the playscript, has been the subject of much controversy ever since Tadeusz Kowzan's pioneering article of 1968.[11] It seems quite arbitrary, though, to decide, as Kowzan does, that a performance consists of thirteen sign systems, or of more or of fewer. Yet to engage in border disputes in that domain seems sterile and hardly likely to be of much methodological significance. One is reminded of Borges's playful taxonomy in *Other Inquisitions,* with its reference to a certain Chinese encyclopedia entitled *Celestial Emporium of Benevolent Knowledge,* in which one is offered the following classification of animals:

> (a) those that belong to the Emperor, (b) embalmed ones, (c) those that are trained, (d) suckling pigs, (e) mermaids, (f) fabulous ones, (g) stray dogs, (h) those that are included in this classification, (i) those that tremble as if they were mad, (j) innumerable ones, (k) those drawn with a very fine camel's hair brush, (l) others, (m) those that have just broken a flower vase, (n) those that resemble flies from a distance.[12]

Borges's antitaxonomy, with its charming logical contradictions, will serve, in a sense, as a cautionary joke, reminding us that all taxonomies and systems, even those less overtly farcical, are more or less arbitrary. My principal concern, therefore, will be not as much with border disputes as with treaties: the ways in which the various components (codes or systems) of a (virtual) dramatic performance are compatible—their combinational norms, in other words.

In examining code focus, I shall, of course, be looking into the ways in which the script itself conveys instructions inscribed within it. Necessarily, any text programs the manner in which it is to be read. But texts are, of course, more or less "open" (to use Umberto Eco's term). Yet playscripts typically are not totally open: in contrast to other literary texts, they may even be overdetermined, especially when the dramatist provides detailed explanations or instructions. Shaw's plays are the prime example—his prefaces are often lengthy studies of his historical, political, or ideological problems arising in his scripts. Contemporary playwrights such as Genet and Beckett provide comprehensive information on how they wish their plays to be performed, including such matters as the precise intonation, diction, or costumes to be used—in other words, a highly detailed frame for the speech acts in their scripts.

Broadly speaking, a first distinction can be drawn between authorial comments inscribed within a playscript and extraneous pronouncements (which I shall not be examining here). Comments contained within a playscript fall under two headings: didascalia (which are, of course, the authorial voice) and glossing comments in the dialogue, which might be termed the metatheatrical function, on the model of Jakobson's metalingual function and on that of the metanarrative function in fiction. I am also excluding from consideration here other hermeneutic constraints that impinge on the playscript, ranging from the intertextual to the social and cultural.

In examining didascalia, then, the problem with which we are concerned is the (habitual) impact of one verbal code (akin to metadiscourse) on the principal verbal code of the playscript (the dialogue). There are four main types of didascalia[13]:

1. Extraneous or extratextual.

2. Autonomous.

3. Technical.

4. "Normal."

These categories (not, I hope, reminiscent of Borges's taxonomy) were determined on the basis of the implied addressee. "Normal" didascalia, contrary to the other types, are, of course, subordinate to the dialogue. When examined according to the same addresser/addressee criterion, didascalia have four main linguistic functions:

1. Attributive (who is speaking?).

2. Addressee (to whom?).

3. Melodic (how? subdivided into emission and reception).

4. Locative (where?).

A further link between didascalia and dialogue is provided by a series of visual codes, including the kinesic, proxemic, and costume.

Although dialogue and didascalia generally work in tandem, there are instances, especially in experimental drama, in which the usually subordinate didascalia acquire a quasi-autonomous function, thereby severing their firm referential bond with the dialogue of which they are supposedly a gloss (though their focus is characteristically the delivery of the dialogue rather than its content, or, to use Benveniste's terminology, *énonciation* as opposed to *énoncé*[14]). Such playwrights as Ring Lardner, J. P. Donleavy, and Eugène Ionesco subvert the convention of subordinate didascalia. In Lardner's *Clemo Uti—"The Water Lilies,"* for example, we read that acts 2 and 3 "were thrown out because nothing seemed to happen."[15] Similarly, in *Cora or Fun at a Spa (An Expressionist Drama of Love and Death and Sex)*, the following stage direction occurs in the middle of the page-length second act: "The

curtain is lowered and raised to see if it will work."[16] In the event that
one were to imagine that Lardner's code was stage directions domi-
nating dialogue, we find the author of the same play undermining his
own convention. After listing the characters, as he puts it, "in the
order in which I admire them,"[17] there is an asterisk placed after the
name of Mrs. Tyler, and the following footnote: "Mrs. Tyler appears
only when one of the other characters is out of the city."[18] Similar
surrealist referential games are at work in the following stage direction at the beginning of Lardner's *Abend di Anni Nouveau,* in which
the waiter coming onstage on horseback "*tethers his mount and lies down
on the hors d'oeuvres. The curtain is lowered and partially destroyed to denote
the passage of four days.*"[19]

There are, needless to say, various ways of setting didascalia referentially loose in addition to the surrealist methods used by Lardner.
Some playwrights allow themselves to be seduced by what might be
termed narrative temptations. Thus, for example, in Donleavy's
plays, stage directions tend to be mostly superfluous from a director's
point of view, and the information provided more of interest to the
reader. In *A Singular Man,* the stage directions appear to belong to a
narrator's discourse, with their frequent focus on Sally Tomson: "*The
reaching out of Miss Tomson's long comforting fingers would save one from
all the ancient deeps of fear, as Smith longingly views that arm so marvelously
exposed this evening from her dazzling dress. . .*"[20] The giveaway is the
deictic expression "this evening." The same character is often referred to elsewhere in the didascalia in ways that reveal the author-
narrator's interest (if not his fixation):

i) "*A gentle rise of chin from this elegant winsome skyscraper
. . .*"[21]

ii) "*Miss Tomson withdrawing her exquisite tootsie under her gown, her
foot searching around for her shoe.*"[22]

iii) "*Miss Tomson . . . looking deeply into the generous Georgian win-
dows of Smith's soul.*"[23]

Amusing flourishes such as "an elegant winsome skyscraper" or an
"exquisite tootsie" can hardly be intended for performance purposes,
nor indeed can one imagine a director (unless he or she is a foot
fetishist) selecting for the cast an actress merely on the basis of her
exquisite tootsie qualifications.

A similar device is to be found in Donleavy's *Saddest Summer of Sam-*

uel S, in which frequent, novelistic reference is made to two characters, Abigail and Samuel S. Abigail, apparently, is distinguished by
her *"fresh fruity fragrance,"*[24] while Samuel S is described in one scene
as *"perceptibly straightening up, like hearing the call to a fire somewhere and
he a member of the local volunteer fire department in a town where this means
you get in on a twice-yearly barbecue."*[25] Needless to say, it would be a
most unusual procedure for a director to flood the auditorium with a
"fresh fruity fragrance" every time Abigail comes onstage! (Though
the other members of the cast could, of course, either hold their noses
or wordlessly convey their delight. . . .)

The cases so far examined, then, are those of stage directions
crying out for release from their normally subservient status; their
regular role is frequently thankless. If they are not rejected outright
by the director, they may be ignored by the reader. The examples
cited are those of didascalia intended for reading and for the reader.
Their role elsewhere can be even bolder, as in Ionesco's *Le Salon de
l'automobile*, in which they are in explicit referential conflict with the
dialogue they are generally supposed to serve. Thus, for example,
the car show salesman's patter, as he shows off a beautiful "jeune voi-
ture blonde" to a potential client, claiming that it has "un moteur
excellent," his comment accompanied by the stage direction *"bruit
d'un moteur défectueux."*[26]

My emphasis in the preceding discussion has been the broad bond
within a playscript between the two constituent levels of discourse,
dialogue and didascalia. Cases of liberated didascalia are, of course,
unusual. Our surprise or amusement when we encounter them demonstrate this. (The effect we have examined is naturally contingent on
reading a playscript; when we see a performance, many of the comic
effects to which I have alluded disappear).

The main problem, however, to which I will address myself here is
code focus (code mesh, if you will), rather than its corollary, code
conflict, which we have so far examined. It need hardly be said that
the manner in which codes mesh is a highly complex business. Some
years ago, Barthes, in a suggestive article, alluded briefly to the problem.[27] I do not claim to solve all aspects of such an important issue in
this short essay. What I hope to provide is no more than a small contribution toward a general theory, in the form of various pointers.
The first question that must be raised is the selection of a suitable
corpus. Obviously, when examining code focus, it is instructive to analyze the opposite device of code conflict—instances of a (normally)

coherent system being made to break down for experimental purposes, as we have seen from a brief consideration of unruly didascalia. Perhaps the most economical way of approaching the issue would be to select a corpus in which there is maximum code mesh. With this principle in mind, therefore, I have chosen a corpus of radio plays.

Radio drama is sometimes thought of as a peripheral subgenre, not worthy of serious consideration, and the lack of theoretical studies bears out this impression. If that is indeed its reputation, it is undeserved, since many major contemporary dramatists, in France, England, and elsewhere, have written significant works in this medium. The roster is impressive; it includes Dylan Thomas, Beckett, Tom Stoppard, Ionesco, Harold Pinter, René de Obaldia, Jean Tardieu—to which one could certainly add many other prominent names.

It hardly need be pointed out that much is eliminated from the radio play, in particular the visual. Only one channel is utilized—the auditory. This does not, of course, mean that the entire realm of the visual (décor, movement, gesture) is cut out. But while radio plays have no visual channel, they convey and represent the visual in other ways, chiefly through the suggestive use of sound. If, in regular drama, space is the crucial element, in radio drama, time is the key dimension. In regular plays, what is represented in front of the audience is necessarily enacted in space. On the radio, the enactment cannot be spatialized in the literal sense; linearity becomes the dominant mode, the possibilities of simultaneity being probably restricted. In radio plays, if the dramatist wishes to tell us that a gesture is being used, for example, he or she must do so either through an explicit comment in the dialogue or through the use of a sound effect. The medium cannot simultaneously transmit an utterance and a gesture, as one can in regular theatre. Space—décor, lighting, props, furniture—cannot just "be" onstage in radio drama as in ordinary plays: space in radio drama has to happen—audibly. Hence the technique of providing an auditory frame with subsequent reminders of location. Several consequences stem from this. Sound effects in radio drama are never to be taken at face value: they must always mean. They generally stand for something else or are linked explicitly to another sign system. Thus, as we shall see, sound may "mean" space, movement, or gesture; it may also "mean" time, as in the obvious example of the striking clock or the cock crowing, signaling dawn in Dylan Thomas's *Under Milk Wood*.

Clearly, then, radio drama, examined from the perspective of the sound dimension, can provide an interesting corpus for theoretical speculation. Let us now explore further how sound works in radio plays. What is heard falls into one of two categories: dialogue (or call it voice, so as to include monologues) and nonvoice. Given the simplification of the theatrical medium inherent in radio drama, both the voice and nonvoice channels must carry more information than they usually do. Thus the dialogue, for example, may contain more references to visual elements than would be necessary in regular drama. Some unaccompanied sound effects are unclear or ambiguous and frequently require a verbal frame.[28] At times, it may be more economical to convey a setting by simply talking about it in the dialogue, or evoking it, as Dylan Thomas does at the beginning of *Under Milk Wood:*

> It is Spring, moonless night in the small town, starless and bible-black, the cobblestones silent and the hunched, courters' and rabbits' wood limping invisible down to the sloe black, slow black crowblack fishing-boat-bobbing sea. The houses are blind as moles (though moles see fine tonight in the snouting, velvet dingles) or blind as Captain Cat there in the muffled middle by the pump and the town clock, the shops in mourning, the Welfare Hall in widows' weeds. And all the people of the lulled and dumbfound town are sleeping now. Hush. . . .[29]

A similar technique is put to good use by Beckett in *All That Fall,* when Mrs. Rooney, reaching the top of the steps after much puffing and panting, is able to take in the whole landscape in front of her: "The entire scene, the hills, the plain, the racecourse with its miles and miles of white rails and three red stands, the pretty little wayside station, even yourselves, yes I mean it, and over all the clouding blue, I see it all, I stand here and see it all. . . ."[30] In both cases, we are dealing with a narrative device, diegetic space,[31] that is, space discursively referred to. In regular drama, diegetic space is often contrasted with mimetic (visually represented) space, as in Genet's *Les Bonnes,* in which Madame's room is the mimetic space, the maids' garret being merely diegetic (and thus never shown).

Dialogue in radio drama can, of course, convey other information besides décor discursively referred to. It can, for example, convey mimetic space with the help of sound effects. In the following example from *All That Fall,* the setting is created by references in the dialogue, the latter acting as a frame for the sound effects:

MRS. ROONEY: All is still. No living soul in sight. There is no one to ask. The world is feeding. The wind—[*brief wind*] scarcely stirs the leaves and the birds—[*brief chirp*] are tired singing. The cows—[*brief moo*]—and sheep—[*brief baa*]—ruminate in silence . . .[32]

The dialogue may also evoke nonstatic visual elements, such as movement (of characters, animals, vehicles), gesture, and costume. Let us consider costume first. It is Mrs. Rooney in the same Beckett play who frequently refers to what she is wearing. References to clothing are usually linked to some other sign system such as sound effects, in the case of a problem:

The wind [*whistling wind*] is whistling through my summer frock as if I had nothing on over my bloomers . . .[33]

or a mishap:

Slocum slams the door. In a scream.
MRS. ROONEY: My frock. You've nipped my frock. [*Mr. Slocum opens the door. Mrs. Rooney frees her frock. Mr. Slocum slams the door.*][34]

or a complaint:

MRS. ROONEY: Am I then invisible, Miss Fitt? Is this cretonne so becoming to me that I merge into the masonry?[35]

Mrs. Rooney's costume-related complaints are not infrequent:

Oh cursed corset! If I could let it out, without indecent exposure. Mr. Tyler! Mr. Tyler! Come back and unlace me behind the hedge![36]

Gesture and facial expression are probably less often referred to than other visual elements such as movement or costume. The corpus of Beckett's radio plays confirms this. Where gesture and facial expression do occur, they tend to be linked to other systems:

1. MRS. ROONEY: Kiss me!

   MR. ROONEY: Kiss you? In public? On the platform? Before the boy? Have you taken leave of your senses?[37]

2. MRS. ROONEY: [*Miss Fitt proffers her arm.*] No, the other side, my dear, if it's all the same to you, I'm left-handed on top of everything else. [*She takes Miss Fitt's right arm.*] Heavens, child, you're just a bag of bones, you need building up.[38]

In the first (aborted) example, gesture and décor are linked; the second is more elaborate, since there is a threeway linkage between gesture, movement, and body. Similarly complex examples in the case of movement, for instance, are often linked to décor. Thus, when Mrs. Rooney, riding in Mr. Slocum's car, exclaims: "Mind the hen!" her exclamation, followed by a scream of brakes, succinctly conveys several pieces of information:

1. The stopping of a previously moving vehicle.

2. The countrified décor (i.e., the hen crossing the road).

3. A reminder that the location of discourse is a passenger car.

The examples cited should suffice to demonstrate that visual elements such as gesture, movement, costume, facial expression, and so forth, do not "exist" in a radio play until explicitly referred to either in the dialogue or, as we shall see, through the use of the other nonvoice channel of radio drama. It is to the latter that we now turn.

Clearly, sound can be used very effectively (and economically) to suggest location. Accordion music was often used to evoke Paris, the striking of Big Ben as a sign for London, and so forth. Signifiers such as these are metonymic or synecdochical. In such instances, we are dealing with a conventional relationship (back to codes again!), equivalent, in the visual domain to, say, a beret standing for French dress (or Frenchness), a bowler hat for British dress, or, metonymically, a picture of the Eiffel Tower as a sign for Paris. In regular plays, this phenomenon could be described as visual synecdoche, or sometimes as visual metonymy. In radio drama, then, we are often dealing with acoustic metonymy or acoustic synecdoche. The economy of this system becomes crucial in radio plays with several changes of location, as in Tardieu's *Candide* (an adaptation of Voltaire's novel).[39] Tardieu makes liberal use of sound effects to suggest the gamut of locations that include Baron Thunder-Ten-Tronck's chateau (evoked by the ticking of a Louis XV clock, the village clock striking, a cock crowing, harpsichord music in the drawing room), outdoor locations on board ship, and thence to Paraguay, represented thus: "*Nous sommes dans une ville du Paraguay. Bruits (autant que possible) 'exotiques'! Par example cris de perroquets. On entend aussi des vendeurs à la criée qui appellent en espagnol: Agua fresca! Buenas galletas!*"[40] In this play, a few sounds suffice to signal a change of place. Sound effects alone, however, are insufficient; they are anchored here as in other plays by an explicit comment in the dialogue preceding or following.

In Beckett's *Embers*, the problem is reversed: instead of constant changes of location as in Tardieu's *Candide,* we find virtual stasis.

Henry, the protagonist, remains in the same location (the beach) for the whole play. The problem, therefore, is to represent an unchanging décor. This is achieved with two devices. The first is the use of an initial frame: "Sea scarcely audible," followed by Henry's comment, "That sound you hear is the sea, we are sitting on the strand. I mention it because the sound is so strange, so unlike the sound of the sea, that if you didn't see what it was, you wouldn't know what it was. . . ."[41] The second device is what might be called the acoustic reminder—the stage directions require the use of the same sea sound effect in all the pauses in Henry's speeches. This example demonstrates the point made earlier that in radio drama a "visual" element is present only when made audible or when the listener is otherwise reminded of it (by verbal reference, for example).

Beckett's *Embers* exemplifies another major sound technique: spatial evocation. There are four instances in the play; two concern Addie (her piano lesson and her riding lesson), and the other two focus on Henry's house and a brief flashback scene between Henry and Ada. The two concerning Addie and the one about Henry's house are especially interesting from a technical point of view. Since they are evocations of areas distinct from the main beach location, they can be categorized, broadly speaking, as diegetic space. But they are not merely verbal references to offstage areas, they are in fact auditory representations of the areas referred to, subordinate to the main dramatic location. They are the radio drama equivalent of the (visible) flashback technique used in regular drama. This is the device used by Sartre, for instance, in *Les Séquestrés d'Altona*, in which the protagonist, Frantz, visibly recalls the past, and in which time is spatialized. Two distinct stage areas are in simultaneous use in those scenes, representing the present and the past. For want of a better term, I called this spatial category mimeticized diegesis [*diégèse mimétisée*] elsewhere.[42] In Beckett's *Embers*, then, space is temporalized, the various locations being transmitted consecutively, since the simultaneous presentation of more than one stage space is not possible in radio drama. In Sartre's play, two axes are used to distinguish events, time—represented by the horizontal plane (the stage areas are marked off by lighting), and space—represented by the vertical plane: Frantz's room upstairs whose discourse is placed in contrast to and in contradiction with that heard downstairs in the drawing room and in Werner's study. In *Embers*, consequently, the spatial sound effects serve a dual purpose—they enable us to differentiate between mimetic space and mimeticized diegetic space; they also enable us to distinguish between two time zones: present (events) and past (evocations).

But sound in radio drama is not used only to evoke space. Its secondary function is to convey other visual elements such as movement. In *Embers,* movement (with the exception of the horses' hooves) is restricted to the beach, so we hear occasional sounds of Henry's boots on the shingle, the slither of the shingle when he sits down, and so forth. When the sound of the sea grows louder, we gather that Henry is nearer the water's edge. The sound level therefore becomes a significant indication of (implied) movement. *All That Fall* is in a sense the antithesis of *Embers,* since movement looms large and numerous sound effects are used to suggest it. Two kinds of sound are predominant: vehicles and footsteps. The former include a horse-drawn cart, a bicycle, a van (which does not stop—its owner therefore does not materialize), a car, and a train. Their use is in each linked to the introduction of a new character—Christy in the cart, Mr. Tyler on the bicycle, Mr. Slocum in the car, and Mr. Rooney on the train. This sound system is closely related to the exposition and enables us to differentiate between characters more clearly, since we tend to link each to his respective vehicle. The footsteps are significant, too. They are at first Mrs. Rooney's; later, the dragging feet, panting, and thudding stick belong to her husband. The sounds represent the efforts required of the aging Mrs. Rooney to get from the village to the station platform to meet her husband's train, and their joint efforts in getting home. If Slocum is referred to, as he drives off, "crucifying his gearbox,"[43] Mrs. Rooney does about the same to her feet, in her efforts to climb the steps up to the station, and lets us know about it. ("[*Sound of her toiling up steps on Miss Fitt's arm*]. This is worse than the Matterhorn, were you ever up the Matterhorn, Miss Fitt, great honeymoon resort. . . . Why don't they have a handrail?"[44]) In *All That Fall,* then, two kinds of movement are conveyed through sound—vehicles moving in relation to Mrs. Rooney; Mr. and Mrs. Rooney's frail efforts to move, in the one case from point A to point B and back, in the other from B to A.

•　　•　　•

It would be premature to draw anything more than tentative conclusions from this preliminary inquiry into stage codes and the rules that govern their combinations and permutations. The corpus of radio plays should have demonstrated the surprising flexibility of an apparently impoverished medium. The important principle it underscores is systemic transformability. Foregrounded dialogue or foregrounded sound effects aided by a verbal frame can represent diegetic or mimetic space or even mimeticized diegetic space, as well as virtually all the other visual codes and systems. The major constraint of the medium, however, is that practically all processes entail consecutive expression: simultaneity (especially spatial simultaneity) is difficult, if not impossible. The final chapter of an inquiry like this remains to be written. Ideally, it would include a complete paradigm of combinational and transformational possibilities.

Finally, I have attempted to clarify the concept of "code." The rules that might be used to establish a hierarchy of codes and systems would be a modified version of Benveniste's criteria for all semiotic systems. These are four in number (four seems to be the magic systemic number): (1) a mode of operation (i.e., a channel); (2) a domain of validity (i.e., where the system must be recognized and obeyed); (3) a limited number of signs; and (4) a relation between the signs giving them a distinct function.[45]

My utopian polysystem would provide the rules that link the three major systems of the drama—theatrical, dramatic, and stage codes—to the various subcodes, those that are specifically dramatic and those that are imported into the medium from other modes of discourse.

NOTES

1. *The Random House Dictionary of the English Language*, ed. Jess Stein (New York: Random House, 1966), 285.

2. Roman Jakobson, "Closing Statement: Linguistics and Poetics," in *Style in Language*, ed. Thomas Sebeok (Cambridge, Mass.: MIT Press, 1960), 350–77, 353.

3. Sebeok, *Style in Language*, 415.

4. See, for example, Catherine Kerbrat-Orecchioni's critique of the Jakobsonian model in her *L'Enonciation. De la subjectivité dans le langage* (Paris: Armand Colin, 1980), 11–33. See also Jacques Dubois's article, "Code, texte, métatexte," *Littérature* 12 (1973): 3–11, which helps clarify the often confused or confusing debate about codes. Umberto Eco provides a useful historical account of the concept of code in a variety of fields, including information theory, cryptography, anthropology, and genetics; see his *Semiotics and the Philosophy of Language* (Bloomington and London: Indiana University Press, 1984), 164–88.

5. Roland Barthes, *S/Z* (Paris: Seuil, 1970), 28.

6. Michael Riffaterre, *Semiotics of Poetry* (Bloomington and London: Indiana University Press), 1978, passim.

7. Riffaterre, *La Production du texte* (Paris: Seuil, 1979) passim. [English translation: *Text Production*, New York: Columbia University Press, 1983].

8. Jonathan Culler, *The Pursuit of Signs* (London: Routledge & Kegan Paul, 1981), 37.

9. Culler, *Structuralist Poetics* (London: Routledge & Kegan Paul and Ithaca: Cornell University Press, 1975), 43.

10. Keir Elam, *Semiotics of Theatre and Drama* (London and New York: Methuen, 1980), 52.

11. Tadeusz Kowzan, "Le Signe au théâtre. Introduction à la sémiologie de l'art du spectacle," *Diogène* 61 (1968): 59–90, reprinted in a revised form in Kowzan, *Littérature et spectacle* (Paris and The Hague: Mouton, 1975), 160–221.

12. Jorge Luis Borges, *Other Inquisitions*, trans. Ruth L. C. Simmes (New York: Simon & Schuster, 1968), 103.

13. See Michael Issacharoff, "Texte théâtral et didascalecture," *MLN* 96, no. 4 (1981): 809–23.

14. Emile Benveniste, "L'Appareil formel de l'énonciation," in his *Problèmes de linguistique générale* II (Paris: Gallimard, 1974), 79–88.

15. *Clemo Uti "The Water Lilies,"* in *The Ring Lardner Reader*, ed. Maxwell Geismar (New York: Scribner's, 1963), 600.

16. *The Ring Lardner Reader*, 617.

17. Ibid., 615.

18. Ibid.

19. Ibid., 619.

20. J. P. Donleavy, *A Singular Man*, in *The Plays of J. P. Donleavy* (New York: Dell, 1972), 283.

21. Ibid., 273.

22. Ibid., 327.

23. Ibid., 353.

24. Ibid., 389.

25. Ibid., 422.

26. Eugène Ionesco, *Le Salon de l'automobile*, in *Théâtre IV* (Paris: Gallimard, 1968), 198.

27. Roland Barthes, "Littérature et signification," in *Essais critiques* (Paris: Seuil, 1964), 258–76.

28. See Roland Barthes's very suggestive article, "Rhétorique de l'image," *Communications* 4 (1964); reprinted in R. Barthes, *L'Obvie et l'obtus* (Paris: Seuil, 1982), 25–42.

29. Dylan Thomas, *Under Milk Wood* (New York: New Directions, 1954), 1.

Michael Issacharoff

30. Samuel Beckett, *All That Fall* (London: Faber & Faber, 1957), 23.

31. For the mimetic/diegetic distinction, see Michael Issacharoff, "Space and Reference in Drama," *Poetics Today* 2, no. 3 (1981): 211–24.

32. Beckett, *All That Fall*, 32.

33. Ibid., 34.

34. Ibid., 15.

35. Ibid., 19.

36. Ibid., 13.

37. Ibid., 27.

38. Ibid., 21–2.

39. Jean Tardieu, *Candide* (Adaptation radiophonique du roman de Voltaire) in *Une soirée en Provence ou le mot et le cri: pièces radiophoniques* (Paris: Gallimard, 1975), 161–205.

40. Ibid., 178.

41. Samuel Beckett, *Embers*, in *Krapp's Last Tape and Other Dramatic Pieces* (New York: Grove Press, 1978), 95–6.

42. See Michael Issacharoff, "Sur les signes des Séquestrés," *Obliques* 18–19 [Sartre] (1979): 141–47.

43. Beckett, *All That Fall*, 17.

44. Ibid., 22.

45. Emile Benveniste, *Problèmes de linguistique générale* II (Paris: Gallimard, 1974), 43–66; see, in particular, 52.

Decoding Mnouchkine's Shakespeare (A Grammar of Stage Signs)

JEAN ALTER

This essay is intended to build bridges between theory and application, semiotics of theatre and sociocriticism. More specifically, I propose to show how Mnouchkine's production of *Richard II* can be made to reveal cultural and social tensions. My assumption is that such a project becomes feasible only when stage signs are articulated within a single and coherent theoretical system.

Theory: Primary and Secondary Stage Signs

I shall assume that stage signs are taken to be those features of production that perform a referential function.[1] I am aware that an intended sign may not be so perceived by the audience; that laxity or variations in codes may disrupt the referential process; that the referent of a given sign will always be somewhat different for each spectator. These are problems in pragmatics, and lie outside my present concern.

I am also aware that a theatre performance cannot, and must not, be reduced to its referential function alone. On the contrary, the very essence of theatre lies in a permanent tension between its referential function, which relies on signs to produce meaning, and what I have called the performant function, which involves no semiotic processes and satisfies the emotional need to witness special achievements: physical, aesthetic, technical, and so on. The functions coexist, competing for attention, and thus, while everything on the stage may indeed become semiotized, as the Prague School suggested, everything may also be desemiotized and turned into a show. Any grammar of stage signs must then take into account the potential variability in referential force.

Finally, I am quite aware that stage signs, and indeed theatre performances, do not exhaust the problems of theatre; that they are but the end product of a complex process that traditionally at least, starts with the production of a given verbal text. Between text and performance, various transformations take place that, I have claimed, are another specific feature of theatre, the condition for permanence and change. The verbal text, of course, once delivered onstage, must be included among the stage signs. However, because of its special power—we always see a play *by* Shakespeare, whoever the director is—I shall keep on referring to it as verbal text, or set of verbal signs, while categorizing all other stage signs as performing signs. Among the latter, no further differentiation seems in order; I am assuming agreement that they belong to multiple semiotic systems.

In fact, there has been much research on such systems, producing both enlightenment and confusion. From the Prague School to Tadeusz Kowzan and to Keir Elam, they have been analyzed, classified, ranked; and their interaction has become a standard topic of semiotic study.[2] That they are cultural and social in origin, found in society at large and then used onstage, has always been acknowledged; but it has also been postulated that, by some magic transubstantiation, once on the stage they become inherently theatrical, thereby constituting the semiotic essence of theatre. As a result, theatre was—and still is—presented as a polysemic medium, where separate colors govern natural language and body language, facial expressions and intonation, choice of color, lighting, clothing, furniture. By the same token, no single grammar of stage signs could be posited, since the very notion of theatre as an autonomous semiotic system has been denied.

Various solutions have been suggested, including Elam's deixis.[3] For my part, I should like to return to the source of confusion. There is no doubt that theatre uses cultural signs, and hence a variety of systems, but not very differently from, say, literature. Yet we agree to recognize that, in literature, a single proper system—natural language—takes care of the primary referential function; and that cultural systems operate only within the space of their decoded referents. When reading *Madame Bovary,* for example, we first move from verbal signs to a fictional world, and then only encounter and decode cultural signs referring to an unfulfilled womanhood in provincial France. Any understanding of *Madame Bovary* is contingent on understanding its linguistic code. The same applies, incidentally, to the verbal text of a play read as literature. I shall argue that theatre performances follow a parallel model, that they have a primary semiotic system, that there is a single specific code governing all stage signs, and that the various cultural systems operate only within the space of the primary referents. I shall further contend that this primary, inherently theatrical, system derives from still another unique feature of theatre: its near total iconicity. Back to Aristotle!

Whether art imitates, distorts, or compensates nature is not in question here. Aristotle's *Poetics* and many theories since merely reflect the awareness that, in theatre, the materiality of all signs, or their signifiers, bears an uncanny and unique resemblance to their referents, or to what they represent. For the most powerful complex sign on stage, the actor speaking his text, this resemblance approaches identity. A staged play, by our semiotic definition, refers to events occurring in a space outside the stage; anything on the stage, when it functions as a sign, refers to something in that space; and the primary code of theatre dictates that outside space, whether visualized in the mind's eye, or concretized as Pavis would have it, be akin to a specular image of the stage, not quite the same but as close as can be. We may fail, or refuse, to form that mirror-image, deny or sabotage the referential function, and concentrate on the performant function carried out *on* the stage, admiring, for example, the acting skills or the handsome features of Laurence Olivier. But as long as we play the semiotic game, we shall visualize a Hamlet who looks, moves, and speaks like a mirror-image of Olivier. In short, the primary system of theatre requires all its signs to have specular referents or, expressed differently, that the form of the signifiers, duplicated by code in the signified, be perceived as the property of the referent that resists individual variations.

The simplicity of a code limited to a specular relation need not concern us. That visible signs—props and scenery—are often not iconic requires explanation, especially, for example, when a plastic cube refers to a chair, an altar, or a coffin, within the same performance. Do we not have a symbol, rather than an icon? We do, of course, but then many codes often accommodate a certain degree of subversion or transgression without losing their pertinence. Thus, all sorts of rhetorical figures, through metaphor or metonymy, enable the so-called poetic language to subvert the standard language code. When Doña Sol tells Hernani: "Vous êtes mon lion, superbe et généreux," she transgresses the conventional meaning of the word. Mademoiselle Mars, an actress of talent but a strict semiotician, rejected the transgression and substituted "seigneur" for "lion" on the opening night; but Hugo the poet knew what he was doing, and he was the greatest of French poets, hélas! Perhaps all poetic quality lies precisely in such subversions that play with the signifiers at the expense of referentiality. And perhaps, for a stage director, poetry is located in symbolic stage signs. But then transgression of the iconic code may serve to interrupt the magic of the referential function for more pedestrian reasons: the alienation effect, conventional commentary, or for the purposes of the performant function.

I can see no other objections to this primary system, which also accounts for the role of cultural, or secondary, systems. The function of cultural signs, evidently, is not primarily theatrical. They are not involved in the semiotic process whereby the stage refers to a space outside; they operate only in that space as sources of meaning and commentary, just as they operate in real life. Were we to encounter Olivier dressed as Hamlet, we would decode his facial expression just as we would Hamlet's and attempt to determine whether he was happy or not.

But even though primary and secondary signs operate in different spaces, performing separate semiotic functions, they are nevertheless mutually interdependent, with common signifiers. Any cultural sign, if it is to function in the space referred to by the stage, must first be placed on the stage; and like everything else onstage, it also functions as a primary sign: that much is self-evident. Cultural signs used to convey meaning generate the choice of primary signs involved in the theatrical process; any resulting problems are pragmatic, calling for the director's judgment and skill. Thus, to show a repulsive Hamlet, the director can choose, instead of Olivier, an ugly hunchback, however risky and original such a decision would be. But the converse relation raises a question of theory: does any primary sign on the stage automatically function as a secondary sign in the space outside? Does any feature of Olivier, decoded as a feature of Hamlet—say, the color of his hair or a turn of the head—have a referent with meaning in some cultural system?

The answer involves two further problems: variations in cultural codes and variations in the complexity of signs. Not everything is covered by cultural codes, even if we seem bent on semiotizing everything, finding signs everywhere. A head turning in response to a call may be interpreted, for example, as betokening civility, interest, or good hearing; but no discrete code operates. A great number of primary signs, a turn of the head as well as shapes or colors of props, would thus not qualify as secondary signs, though individual interpretations remain unpredictable. But what about all primary signs that do not fall into some category covered by a cultural system? Will they necessarily operate as (potential) secondary signs? Now, some systems have tight, normative codes, such as the highway code; others are loose and fragmentary. The color system, for one, codifies red as standing for passion and life, and black for despair and death. Ideally, a red dress on a young woman, a black dress on an old woman, would function as strong cultural signs, typical of a given referent. Beige, however, is not clearly coded and therefore not precise in its meaning. Yet a beige dress on an old woman would usually be acceptable, whereas a red dress would not; to that extent, it seems to me, it would function as a cultural sign, albeit vaguely. To mark this difference, I shall refer to "typical" signs as *active,* and to "acceptable" signs as *passive.* Most primary signs will function as either active or passive cultural signs, and their specific choice will result in an outside space full of meaning, or flat, or selectively stressing some meaning.

The relation between primary signs and cultural signs also depends on the interplay between simple and complex signs. Most primary signs are perceived as distinctly complex—that is, as aggregates of simple signs. Actors use gesture, facial expression, intonation, movement, costume, and whatnot; props involve shape, size, color, texture. Varying degrees of complexity will be reflected in the specular space outside; it will be full of details if many complex primary signs appear on the stage. By the same token, however, the potential for the operation of secondary signs can be increased or decreased; a cluttered interior or costume will trigger more cultural codes than a bare stage with a white backdrop or nudity. Meaning is implicit, but not automatically the result of an increase or decrease in complexity. A large number of primary signs may function passively, and a few active signs may convey explicit meaning.

Finally, in order to articulate this grammar, I had to postulate that there are no complex secondary signs, that cultural systems code only simple signs, and that any *gestalts* with meaning we perceive can al-

ways be divided into independent components. A short tight red
dress, with décolleté and slit, has a definite referent, but in fact each
of its elements points individually to that referent. I must acknowledge, however, one very important exception: a special cultural system, the system of theatre conventions, not only admits but also
favors complex conventional signs that, as indivisible units, refer to
some theatrical tradition: set characters, set gestures, set movements,
set sets. A concerted use of such signs obviously theatricalizes theatre,
through a double referential focusing on theatre; as cultural signs,
they suggest that the space outside has a theatrical meaning, and as
primary signs, they define that space as that of theatre.

Mnouchkine's *Richard II*

Mnouchkine's *Richard II* opened in 1982 at the Cartoucherie, a theatre reputed for its innovative productions, reasonably leftist ideology, excellent acting, and sparse sets. The play was a hit, and not only
among snobs; by all accounts, it was the play of the season. In July, it
moved to the Cours des Papes, the centerpiece of the Avignon theatre
festival, as the prize offering of the French cultural establishment. In
1982–83, it returned to Paris to play to full houses. The key to this
success is Mnouchkine's bold decision to stage Shakespeare in the kabuki style. What follows is an account of how it worked the evening I
saw the play.

When first summoned, by a clash of cymbals, the actors ran on,
costumed as Japanese samurai in ample yellow, red, and green silk
robes, curved swords at their sides; they pranced twice around the
stage, bare but for a platform in the middle, then formed a semicircle,
squatting on presumably bowed legs hidden beneath their skirts,
while their apparent leader, leaping on the platform, took the hieratic
stance of a Japanese warlord: freeze and applause. Then Shakespeare's words, in a good French translation, began to weave their
fable. Surprisingly, the delivery was not sacrificed to the visual effects,
or to the cymbals and drums backstage; on the contrary, the text was
declaimed as it might have been at the Comédie Française, with a
clarity as uncompromising as the stylization of the facial expressions,
heavily accentuated like masks, and the ritual postures of the pseu-
dosamurai. The referential space of the verbal signs was thus explicitly located in fourteenth-century England, while the equally

prominent performing signs could be taken to represent medieval Japan.

And why not? said the critics, echoing Mnouchkine. Both countries had lived through the same decadent feudalism, with power struggles and family bloodbaths. The kabuki style thus offered a proper visual metaphor for the society in Shakespeare's play; and the samurai was a natural symbolic sign for an English lord. The massive subversion of the iconic code was thus justified by specific thematic resemblances. And why was it undertaken at all? It was needed, according to Mnouchkine, to regenerate the worn-out staging conventions of the West through the injection of new forms. The kabuki was to rejuvenate the Shakespearean tradition.

Coming from Mnouchkine, so innovative in the past (*1789, 1793, L'Age d'or*), this recourse to borrowing was rather surprising. In terms of her own argument, furthermore, it was paradoxical if not downright contradictory. If, indeed, existing theatrical conventions had to be discarded as conventions, why substitute other conventions that, however exotic, flaunted their conventional nature? Was the play on, or with, conventions the real object of the game, and the text but a pretext?

The treatment of Shakespeare's text and kabuki forms involved a similar paradox. To be sure, it did show respect for the integrity of each set of signs. Yet depriving both of their natural—that is, iconic—complements, it also showed indifference to their full potential as signs. Mnouchkine had formed a two-headed monster, whose heads spoke in unison but in different tongues; and however intriguing or pleasing their duet (or duel), a single voice would have been more effective; but perhaps nothing important was to be conveyed?

Both paradoxes clearly reflect some ambivalence about the referential function of theatre, on the one hand protected, on the other undermined. A similar attitude seems to have motivated Mnouchkine's radical polarization of primary signs between minimal and maximal complexity. Sets and props were confined to a few backdrops and a couple of symbols; in striking contrast, actors bore many precise signs. By virtue of the iconic code, the audience was thus offered a very neutral mirror-space, where the only distinct elements were samurailike figures behaving in a samurailike manner—normally, an invitation to visualize and fill that space with samurai-related features. At the same time, however, the verbal text insisted that the space be filled with England-related features. A proliferation of complex props or sets would have forced a choice between the conflicting visualizations, ending in the subordination of one space to another, England to Japan or vice versa. Mnouchkine's self-imposed sobriety thus protected the balance between the referential processes of verbal and performing signs. Nevertheless, since she prevented both groups of signs from forming a detailed and, therefore, convincing mirror-space, she succeeded in undermining both referents, England and Japan.

Such contradictions would be bothersome if real. But closer attention to a grammar of signs permits me to dispel them. Until now, I have followed the critics' assumption that, by massive subversion of iconicity, the kabuki samurai functioned as symbolic signs for English lords. This assumption, however, was rooted in a confusion between the roles or primary and secondary signs; in fact, Mnouchkine's claims to the contrary notwithstanding, no basic subversion occurred. Indeed, by normal operation of the primary code, for the sophisticated Parisian audience the specular images of kabuki figures were not samurai, but kabuki figures—that is, kabuki actors costumed like samurai and performing in a special style. This is what the spectators were prepared to see, and saw. The mirror-space outside, conveyed by kabuki signs, never was medieval Japan, but rather a stage on which kabuki actors performed.

By the same token, the dichotomy of verbal and performing signs, and related paradoxes, were resorbed in a unified process. All primary signs converged on a single referent: the specular stage on which kabuki actors performed *Richard II*. Mnouchkine's actors were not kabuki, but signs for kabuki actors and the Cartoucherie a sign for a kabuki stage: a theatre-within-a-theatre strategy carried to the extreme. As usual in such situations, the verbal text retained its referential power: *Richard II* performed by kabuki actors still referred to its own specular space on the specular stage of performance. In that sense, the referential function of theatre was upheld.

A risk of desemiotization was implicit in the psychological impact of the experiment. When the main referent is a performance, the very notion of performance is promoted as the proper object of theatre; and the interest in the performant function is maximized. Why stage a kabuki performance of Shakespeare if not to draw attention to aesthetics, skill, and novelty in the use of stage signs, specifically in the kabuki style but also in general? The interest in *Richard* is proportionally downgraded, with the resulting threat to the referential function. Hence a new paradox: since the kabuki performance had to be a good performance of *Richard II*, to justify its presence, it also had to ensure a protection against the threat to referentiality. The foregrounding of performing signs was potentially counterproductive in that perspective, and the importance attached to the clear delivery of Shakespeare's lines must not have seemed to Mnouchkine to be a sufficient antidote; for suddenly, in the last act, she discarded the kabuki convention: a naked man in a cage was brought on the stage to voice Richard's final soliloquy. At that moment, verbal and performing signs coalesced in a single space and a powerful referentiality. But to what, and to whom? Not to fourteenth-century England, nor to its miserable king. Out of an historic context, the naked man in the cage offered a universal sign referring to all men stripped to their bare condition, and about to die. Now, this is strong stuff, and guaranteed to work on the most cynical bourgeois audience, always eager to identify with universals and forget History. Sweating their purge, emotional needs satisfied, the spectators felt that they had had a great theatrical experience and were ready to attribute it to the seductive kabuki performance. Mnouchkine's *Richard II* was a moving and beautiful production, whatever its meaning.

If the meaning was thus forgotten, or lost, it must have been that the cultural signs, which were intended to provide it, did not function properly. It remains to be seen by what strategies Mnouchkine's signs managed to play down their referentiality and, in the first place, how her choice of primary signs undercut the potential of the secondary systems.

Shakespeare's texts are rich in cultural signs. A French translation may reduce the wealth, but at least what survives is communicable. The French, like the Anglo-Saxons, enjoy debating the meaning of *Hamlet* or *Othello*. But Mnouchkine chose one of Shakespeare's historical dramas, which, on the Continent, become more opaque. *Richard II*, in particular, with its convoluted family relations, dynastic problems, location shifts, loyalties, and precedences, is difficult to decode. Parisians may have some idea of what is going on, but it is unlikely that they will have a real feeling for the meaning of events, unless, of course, they are helped by cultural signs supplied onstage by the director. The kabuki gambit, precluding any such support from familiar cultural sources, increased the opacity. Still, a few systems escaped: lighting, voice, intonation. It is significant that in each case Mnouchkine favored the passive signs, those coded as acceptable for the complex referent, but not typical, not noticeable, not disclosing any meaning. I remember no particular light, in contrast to so many in Vitez's *Hamlet,* no particular voice; as for intonation, only the clarity and forcefulness stood out, referring to Shakespeare's text as a text to be declaimed, not as a source of meanings to be modulated. *Richard II*'s specular image for the Cartoucherie's audience must have been, I suspect, like a tale full of sound and fury, signifying nothing. But *Richard II* as a poetic text came across clearly.

It was the kabuki element, the performing signs, however, that were especially memorable; nothing distracted from them; no cultural signs suggested a decoding of their meaning. No doubt the kabuki convention, like much of our worn-out Western tradition, uses complex theatrical signs that, through ritualized gestures and costumes, convey a meaning. Nonetheless, to a Parisian audience unaware of that code, kabuki conventions are as opaque as the Japanese language. The referential function had no chance at all, and, by default, the performant function took over.

How does all this serve sociocriticism? Evidently, Mnouchkine is not at issue (despite the striking differences between this and her earlier productions); one must believe in her sincerity and genuine intention to stage *Richard II* with equal regard for referential and performant functions. The downgrading of referentiality is all the more important because it reveals a social pressure at work, not only the feeling that it is better to show than to tell, but also that showing does not need to tell anything, that telling is superfluous and perhaps impossible. Of course, this feeling does not merely reflect the current emphasis on the visual; images also tell. What happens on Mnouchkine's stage, and on many others, may also be seen in some comic strips in which the story, increasingly weak or incoherent, serves merely to support impressive graphics: the indifference to meaning is the same. What social tension can be the cause?

A clue lies in the few referential processes that Mnouchkine spared. The only surviving referents, we have seen, were a kabuki performance of *Richard II* in the specular space, *Richard II* as a literary text, and the kabuki theatrical conventions as meanings conveyed by the cultural systems. All three were obviously resistant to the semiotic capacities of the Paris audience. In that sense, they illustrate the general frustration of a society that finds it increasingly difficult to decode its own signs, which slide into obsolescence at an increasingly rapid rate;

a bad case of "future shock." But suppose decoding were possible, for a happy few. The meaning would be the meaning of a theatrical performance, a literary text, a theatre performance, and not the meaning of reality; it would at best say something about an artistic product, labeled and packaged as such, an already formally coded representation of reality. This implies more than frustration: it implies total semiotic alienation from reality, where signs refer only to other signs, formally fixed in the past. No wonder deconstruction turns against signs; this is the age of semiotic malaise. Other forms of communication thrive: mystical and aesthetic communion, emotional appeals and responses, performant functions. This is not the place to name the social causes of this state of affairs; I have tried to do so elsewhere. Suffice it to say that artists, in such a world, turn away from reality toward the safe art forms of the past, joining critics who have been doing likewise.

NOTES

1. For a discussion of the referent in theatre, see Jean Alter, "Waiting for the Referent: Waiting for Godot?" in *On Referring in Literature,* ed. Anna Whiteside and Michael Issacharoff (Bloomington: Indiana University Press, 1987).

2. See, for example, Matejka and Titunik, eds., *Semiotics of Art. Prague School Contributions* (Cambridge: Mass.: MIT Press, 1976); Tadeusz Kowzan, "Le signe au théâtre. Introduction à la sémiologie de l'art du spectacle," *Diogène* 61 (1968): 59–70; Keir Elam, *The Semiotics of Theatre and Drama* (London and New York: Methuen 1980).

3. Elam, *The Semiotics of Theatre and Drama,* 72–4.

From Text to Performance

PATRICE PAVIS

Examining the ways in which a text culminates in a performance is complicated by the fact that when the production is finally made available to the spectator, it is already too late to watch the preparatory work of the director; his or her product, in which the text is only one of the several components, is already finished. It is not possible to deduce from the performance the work that led up to it; for the performance is the synchronic confrontation of signifying systems, and it is their interaction, not their history, that is offered to the spectator and that produces meaning.

I shall therefore not speak of the director, a private individual instructed by the theatrical institution to put a name to the artistic product, but of *mise en scène,* defined as the bringing together or confrontation, in a given space and time, of different signifying systems, for an audience. Mise en scène is here taken to be a structural entity, a theoretical subject or object of knowledge. Since the director, the "unknown father," is not directly relevant to us here, he will be replaced (with apologies to practitioners) by the structural notion of mise en scène.

It is important to distinguish between: (1) the dramatic text, the verbal script that is read or heard in performance; (2) the performance, all that is made visible or audible on stage, but not yet perceived or described as a system of meaning, or as a pertinent relationship of signifying stage systems; and (3) the mise en scène, the confrontation of dramatic text and performance. Mise en scène is not an empirical object, the haphazard assembling of materials, the ill-defined activity of the director and his or her stage team before the performance; it

86

is an object of knowledge, a system of associations or relationships uniting the different stage materials, forged *in* performance.

The distinction made between mise en scène as an empirical object and as an object of knowledge allows one to reconcile the aesthetics of production and reception. Indeed, mise en scène, as a structural system, exists only when received and reconstructed by a spectator from the production. To decipher the mise en scène is to receive and interpret the system created by an artistic team. The aim is not one of reconstructing the intentions of the director, but of understanding as a spectator the system elaborated by those responsible for the production.

For our present purposes, mise en scène will be taken to be that of a playscript, not one syllable of which may be changed by the director, and constituting, therefore, one in a series of interpretations of a fixed text. Examples will be taken from recent productions of plays by Marivaux.

The definition of mise en scène as a structural notion does not tell us which system one can derive from a performance, or whether it is even possible to establish a general theory for the mise en scène of seventeenth- or eighteenth-century theatre. The formulation of the problems and scope of a semiotics of mise en scène simply provides a tool for testing such a theory.

At this stage in theatre semiotics, nothing warrants our linking semiotics of the text and that of the performance. In fact, they are distinct both in the methodologies they employ and in their respective aims. Thus, even in the study of a playscript, it is essential to specify whether it is being approached as a text or as a constituent part of a particular production.

Mise en scène is not the staging of a supposed textual "potential." It does not consist in finding stage signifieds for the verbal signs of the text; this would necessarily amount to no more than a superfluous repetition of the text itself. It would entail disregarding the signifying materiality of the verbal and stage signs and positing theatrical signifieds capable of setting aside their signifying matter, and eliminating any difference between the verbal and the nonverbal. Any theatrical semiotics that presupposes that the dramatic text has an innate theatricality, a matrix for production or even a score, which must be extracted at all costs and expressed on the stage, implying that the playscript can and should exist, as it were, verbatim in performance, seems to be begging this question. Those who hold this position would contend that every play has only one good mise en scène already present in the text. Marivaux, for example, has long been thought of in terms of how his plays have been staged at the Comédie-Française, all bustling activity and stilted diction—known superficially as *marivaudage*, which was considered to be the essential characteristic to be emphasized in production.

Mise en scène does not need to be faithful to a dramatic text. The notion of faithfulness, a cliché of critical discourse, stems in fact from confusion. Faithfulness to what? If it be to an acting tradition (often obscure in the case of French classicism), the criterion is irrelevant. If, however, to produce a faithful mise en scène is to repeat, or believe one can repeat, the text on stage, what would be the point of a production at all?

Different mises en scène of a common text, particularly those produced at very different moments in history, do not provide readings of the same text; for the "text" is the result of a process that we shall call, with Ingarden and Vodička, its concretization.[1] Nevertheless, the text is not an unstructured reservoir of signifieds, a *Baumateriel* (building material), as Brecht would say. The text is indeed the very reverse: the result of an historically determined process of concretization—signifier (work-as-thing), signified (aesthetic object), and *Social Context* (an abbreviation for what Mukarovsky calls the "total context of social phenomena, science, philosophy, religion, politics, economics, etc. of the given milieu")[2] are variables that modify the concretization of the text, variables definable by their variability. During the last twenty years, Marivaux has been subject to this variability, to the great displeasure of philologists who regard themselves as the guardians of the Marivaux heritage; the plays performed were always unabridged, but variations in the *Social Context* (in the dramaturgical analyses of the texts, as well as in the ideological configuration of the audience) were such that concretizations of the mises en scène always seemed to these "inspectors" unfaithful to texts too long held captive by their tradition of *marivaudage* and *la surprise de l'amour*.

Mise en scène is not the stage representation of the textual referent, nor is it the visual concretization of the "holes" in the text or of a textual score that needs a performance in order to take on meaning. Any text, not just a dramatic text, has holes; in other respects, however, it can be "too full," or overloaded. Rather than try to find these empty or overloaded areas, one should try to understand the processes of determination and indetermination: mise en scène merely performs the function of "emptying" or "filling."

The result is that mise en scène is not the fusion of two referents (textual and stage) and does not strive to find their common denominator. In Lassalle's production of *Les Fausses confidences,* for example, Araminte says: "What! Are you not going to the table?" Marivaux's corresponding stage direction specifies: "*Dorante does not go towards the table.*" Lassalle's production contains no visible table. The referent of Araminte's speech therefore is not represented by an identifiable object such as a table: mise en scène does not have to furnish a referent object. However, the spectator is quite capable of imagining a table (hidden, as in Lassalle's production, or forgotten, or in the mind's eye). Thus we have here a discursive referent that obliges the spectator to construct from the text alone the referent object that a realistic mise en scène would not have failed to represent visually, giving the illusion that the textual referent, as well as the stage referent, was actualized on the stage.

Mise en scène is not the performative realization of the text. Contrary to what Searle believes, the actors do not have to carry out the instructions of the text and the stage directions, as though these had the illocutionary force of a "cake recipe," in order to produce a stage performance.[3] Are not the most outstanding productions those in which the mise en scène has invented a completely different speech-act context, ignoring the playwright's few instructions with regard to the manner of speaking certain lines or playing a scene?

Finally, mise en scène is not obliged to follow stage directions. Stage directions concerning the circumstances of utterances are not the ultimate truth of the text, a formal command to produce the text in such a manner, or even an indispensable shifter between text and performance. Their textual status is uncertain. Do they constitute an optional extratext? A metatext that determines the dramatic text? Or a pretext that suggests one solution before the director decides on another? The evaluation of their status cannot be divorced from history; although one should not forget that they form part of authorial speech, it should be remembered that the producer has the choice of either using them or not, as in the case of Gordon Craig, who considered stage directions an insult to his freedom. To conclude, it would seem inappropriate to accept stage directions, within the framework of a theory of mise en scène, as absolute directives. Let us now turn to mise en scène and the links between text and performance.

Patrice Pavis

Mise en scène as a Means of Modulating the Relationship Between Text and Performance

Instead of defining the relationship between text and performance as one of conversion, translation, or reduction of the one to the other, I will attempt to describe it as a way of establishing meaning and as the balance between opposing semiotic systems, such as verbal and non-verbal, symbolic and iconic, statement and utterance, or as the result of clashes between incompatible semiological principles, for the greater theoretical amusement of onlookers.

Stage Utterances

Mise en scène tries to provide the dramatic text with a context of utterance that will give meaning to statements. Statements in the playscript seem therefore to be the product of (stage) utterance and at the same time the text used by the mise en scène to envisage a context of utterance in which the text acquires meaning. Mise en scène is not a transformation of text into performance, but rather a theoretical "fitting" that consists in putting the text under dramatic and stage stress, in order to test how stage utterance challenges the text and initiates a hermeneutic circle between statements for delivery and utterance, thus opening up the text to several possible interpretations.

In recent Marivaux productions, the texts were rediscovered because directors like Patrice Chéreau, Jacques Lassalle, and Daniel Mesguich dared to force the lines into new contexts of utterance, by modifying tempo or gesture, or by creating unexpected spatial relations. This fresh utterance of the script uncovered what had been repressed for a long time, in fact from the very beginning. Who would have believed it possible in staid old France? Marivaux's texts began to abound in new meanings, even to excess.

The Concretization Circuit

The change in context of utterance goes hand in hand with a renewed concretization of the dramatic text; a two-way relationship is established between the dramatic text and the *Social Context*. Today, the text is placed in a context of utterance according to the new *Social*

Context of its reception, which allows or facilitates a new analysis of the *Social Context* of the textual and stage production, which in turn modifies the analysis of the text and so on, ad infinitum. This theoretical "fitting," this discrepancy between text and stage, the disparity between the reading of yesterday's *Social Context* and that of today, constitute the mise en scène. The latter is a possibility for stage utterance, leading to a fresh text; it is always in a state of becoming, since it does no more than point the way, preparing the text for utterance while adopting a wait-and-see attitude.

Verbal Versus Nonverbal: Reading Actualized

Mise en scène is reading actualized: the dramatic text no longer has an individual reader, but a *possible collective* reading, the result of the textual concretization and concretization per se, namely the stage concretization. Mise en scène is always a parable on the impossible exchange between the verbal and the nonverbal: the nonverbal (e.g., staging) makes the verbal text talk, reduplicating its utterance, as if the dramatic text, by being uttered on stage, were able to comment on itself, without the help of another text, by giving prominence to what is said and what is shown. Thus mise en scène speaks by showing and not by speaking, with the result that irony and denegation (Freud's *Verneinung*) are its usual mode of existence. Another hermeneutic circle is formed by mise en scène as denegation: the mise en scène of the text speaks without speaking, through stage representation (which is comparable to dream representation), staging in turn enriches and gives a reading of the text. Even the simplest and most explicit mise en scène always succeeds in making a text say what a critical text would be incapable of saying: literally the inexpressible.

Although little is known at present about nonverbal processes of communication (kinesics, proxemics, perception of rhythm and voice quality), even such limited knowledge can throw some light on the work of the actor, whose nonverbal behavior has so great an influence on the spectator's understanding of the accompanying text. Some study has already been done on the question of tempo in the playscript. John Styan, for instance, has indicated the importance of textual rhythm: "Movement, tempo and mood are not the qualities in a play that are most readily recognized from the printed text, but they are elements without which the drama would not hold."[4] Currently, producers especially Vitez, are exploring this dimension, emphasizing different tempos through the mise en scène, thus producing quite divergent concretizations.

Change in Perspective

The preceding remarks indicate a clear change of perspective, a desire to get away from a logocentric notion of theatre, with the text as the central and stable element and mise en scène necessarily an incidental transcription thereof.

Until certain postmodernist experiments, in which the text was considered to be asemantic material to be manipulated by such processes as ready-mades, collages, quotation, and concrete poetry, both the fiction and the mise en scène seemed to pivot around the dramatic text. The most recent experiments in postmodernism on the nonverbal element and the new status these have accorded the text—that of a sound pattern and a signifying rhythmic structure—have not been without repercussion on the conception of the French classical drama and its mise en scène, which no longer always turns on the semantic pivot of the text. Thus, in his production of *La dispute*, Chéreau centered his mise en scène on the separation of the observers' space and the adolescents' space. The hyperreal set, manipulated from within by unseen stagehands, and the actors' gestures and body movements created an all-powerful framework in which the text unfolded; actions and stage images were upgraded to signifying systems, centralizing and reassembling all other systems. The mise en scène brought about a reversal of the traditional sequence of text → fictionalization → performance. But this reversal is exceptional and texts continue to be *read*.

In speaking of mise en scène, it is useful to distinguish between three kinds of reading:

1. The reading of the text as carried out by an ordinary reader, the kind of thing a spectator might do before going to see a performance. The problem here is to ignore the context of the text as a stage utterance.

2. The reading of the performance, taking account of the mise en scène as a system of meanings.

3. The reading of the connection specifically established by the mise en scène between the first two kinds of reading. This is the reading of the dramatic text as carried out by those participating

in the mise en scène. Let us pause to consider this third kind of reading, in Ingarden's or Vodička's terms, the stage concretization stemming from the textual concretization.

Metatext and Concretization

In order to conceptualize the concretization of the dramatic text by the mise en scène, we as spectators must look for the director's metatext—that is, the commentary on the text or the stage version he or she offers. The problem lies in locating this metatext of the mise en scène: nowhere does it exist as a separate and complete text; it is disseminated in the choice of acting style, scenography, rhythm. Moreover, according to our conception of mise en scène, it exists only when it is recognized and, in part, shared by the audience. More than a performance text beside the dramatic text, the metatext is what organizes, from within, the scenic concretization, thus not being *beside* the dramatic text, but, as it were, *inside* it, being the result of the concretization circuit (signifier, *Social Context*, and signified of the text).

A normative, and even political, question arises: must this metatext be easy to recognize and formalize, in the form of a battery of explicit options and theses? Or must it on the contrary be discreet and even secret, being mainly the product of the spectator? Perhaps it is simply both at once! Mise en scène would appear to be a paradox, existing only when the spectator chooses to recognize it, being there without intruding, even seeming to be nothing but the creative projection of the spectator.

Three related questions are crucial in attempting to determine the circuit formed by the dramatic text and the *Social Context*.

1. What concretization is made of the dramatic text with every new reading or mise en scène, and what circuit of concretization is established between the work-as-thing, the *Social Context*, and the aesthetic object?

2. What fictionalization, or production of fiction from text and stage, results from the combined effects of the text and the reader, the stage and the spectator? In what way is the interaction of the two fictions, textual and stage, essential to theatrical fictionalization?

3. What ideologization is applied to the dramatic text and the performance? The text, that of the script or the performance,

can only be understood intertextually, when confronted with the discursive and ideological structures of a period or of a corpus of texts. The dramatic and the performance texts must be considered in relation to the *Social Context*—that is, other texts and discourses about reality produced by a society. This relationship being the most fragile and variable imaginable, the same dramatic text readily produces an infinite number of readings.

Of the three questions, that of the theory of fiction and its mediatory role in the relationship between text and performance is central to any research on mise en scène and merits further discussion here.

Textual Fictionalization Versus Stage Fictionalization

The theory of fiction entails examining the relationship between text and performance from the perspective of fictionalization generated by mise en scène for the audience. Fiction can appear to be the mediating element between what the dramatic text says and what the performance shows, as if mediation could be achieved by the textual and visual representation of a possible fictional world, constructed first of all by dramaturgical analysis and reading, and subsequently represented by being staged. This is not far from the truth, provided that one does not surreptitiously reintroduce the theory of the actualized referent as the embodiment of this mediation. If there is indeed an obvious relationship between text and performance, it does not take the form of a translation or reduplication of the former by the latter, but rather it takes the form of a transformation or confrontation of a fictional universe structured by the text and a fictional universe produced by the performance. The modalities of this confrontation need further examination.

The two fictional states, that of the text and that of the performance, have their own peculiarities, although it is to be understood that (1) the fictional universe of the performance encompasses and permeates the fictional universe of the text uttered on stage, furnishing it with a specific context of utterance; and (2) the fictional universe of the performance is liable to be at any moment contradicted and broken up from within by the text uttered in performance. This dramatic text is a precise and easily accessible semiotic system. Since it is verbal, it offers linguistically tangible signifieds onto which the other signifying systems can graft their messages.

The confrontation of the two fictional modes takes place in a theatrical production, through a two-layered fictional channel, consisting of (1) stage fictionalization, in utterance the visible and audible context of the dramatic text; and (2) textual fictionalization, performed by the receiver, who is free to construct a fiction other than that chosen by the mise en scène, and to treat the text as an entity accessible through imagination, through "the mind's eye," to quote Hamlet.

This very real distinction between the two fictions is nevertheless purely theoretical, for they intersect and merge for the delight and illusion of the spectator. The stage and its representation of locality and space immediately create a setting that claims to be the scene of the fiction, the mimesis of the fictional world. This first stage fictionalization is strengthened by the actors, the atmosphere, and the rhythm, all doing their utmost to persuade us that they incarnate the fiction. The stage fictionalization totally "cements" the textual fiction (sometimes even seeming to be the incarnation of the word, the only possible mise en scène). The two fictions eventually merge so completely that we no longer know whether the dramatic text has created the context of utterance or the utterance has engendered the text heard, it seeming impossible for it to engender any other text. The fusion of the two fictional states seems designed to confirm and intensify the spectator's illusion that he or she is in a foreign fictional world, so much so that what the spectator sees in front of him or her (an actor, lighting or sound effect) seems to exist elsewhere, on some "other plane."

This dual process of distancing and reconciliation is not the result of chance or the miracle of illusion. It is the work of mise en scène, a machine that can accommodate different fictional systems and modulate a fictional system according to the available space and the audience's expected perception. The art of mise en scène consists, in practical terms, of taking into account the different systems and cutting up space according to optical laws that turn the stage into a Platonic cave in which shadows and make-believe objects pass for real and vice versa, in which materials are accumulated, arranged, and enriched until the said cave becomes, in the eyes of the fascinated audience, Ali Baba's.

The fusion of the two fictions, which could be considered one of the specific features of theatrical perception, stems (at least for the mise en scène of a preexisting dramatic text) from the exchange or dialectic between two semiotic principles concerning the linguistic text and stage representation:

1. The linguistic text, by the very nature of its (linguistic) signs, has meaning as an *absence* for a *presence*—that is, an absent fictional world experienced as present and real.

2. The stage claims to be an immediate presence of what is in fact only an absence and the confusion between a signifier and a referent. (The so-called referent is in fact only a discursive referent or rather a signifier that gives the illusion of being a referent.)

Mise en Scène as Discourse on Hiatus and Ambiguity

The confrontation of the two fictions not only establishes links between text and utterance, absence and presence, it also contrasts indeterminacy and ambiguity in the text and in the performance. These areas do not necessarily coincide. Sometimes the performance can make a passage in the text ambiguous, polysemic, or devoid of meaning. At other times, however, the performance can resolve a textual contradiction or indeterminacy. Similarly, the dramatic text can eliminate ambiguities in the performance, or, conversely, introduce new ones; this occurs whenever the hearer of the text seeks, in the performance, confirmation or contradiction of textual signifieds stemming from the concretization circuit.

One of the reasons for the renewal of Marivaux has been the deliberate effort of mise en scène to make opaque or polysemic what had always been accepted as clear in the text: the love situations had certainly been seen as confusing, but only for the heroes and only momentarily. In productions by Chéreau and Lassalle, the acting—close to the language of action in *La dispute* or restricted to Dorante's closed, cold, and inscrutable expression in *Les fausses confidences*— breaks with the former clarity of behavior regarded as being in conflict only with the character's conscience.

To make opaque on stage what was clear in the text or to clarify what was opaque: such operations of determinacy/indeterminacy are typical of mise en scène. Usually, mise en scène is an interpretation, an *explication de texte*, bringing about a mediation between the original receiver and the present-day receiver. Sometimes, however, it is a *com-*

plication de texte, a deliberate effort to prevent any communication between *Social Contexts* of the two receptions.

In certain productions, those inspired by Brechtian dramaturgical
analysis, for instance, the mise en scène can show how the dramatic
text is itself an imaginary solution to real ideological contradictions
that existed at the time the fiction was invented. Mise en scène, then,
has the task of making it possible to imagine and stage the textual
contradiction. In productions concerned with the revelation of a
Stanislavskian kind of subtext, the unconscious element of the text is
supposed to accompany, in a parallel text, the continuous and in itself
pertinent flow of the text actually spoken by the characters.

Whatever may be the reason, overt or otherwise, for wanting to
show the contradiction in the fable or the profound truth of the text
through the revelation of its subtext, mise en scène is always a discourse beside a flat and neutral reading of the text; it is—in the etymological sense of the word—parodic. But neither the contradiction
nor the unconscious subtext is actually beside the text or above it (like
the metatext); both are to be found in the collision of the two readings, within the concretization, the fictionalization, the relationship to
ideology, just as a parody cannot be separated from the subject par-
odied.

A Typology of Mises en Scène

The theory of mise en scène discussed here allows us to eschew impressionistic discourse on the style, inventiveness, and originality of
the director adding his or her personal touch to a precious text regarded as closed and inviolate. However, the same theory is more or
less incapable of giving answers to two very frequent questions:

1. Is the mise en scène faithful? (We have seen that this question
is meaningless, for it is based on presuppositions regarding the
fixed meaning of the text.)

2. Which mises en scène could a given dramatic text receive and
what different kinds of mise en scène are available?

In order to answer this second question, and to avoid resorting to
the naive dichotomy of faithfulness/unfaithfulness of the first question, the semiotician can but examine how mise en scène, in the form
of a performance text, is determined according to the following

modes: autotextual, intertextual, and ideological (or rather ideotextual). These three dimensions, which I have defined elsewhere[5] as the three components or levels of any text, coexist in any mise en scène. The purpose of the proposed typology is to examine the emphasis accorded to one of these three dimensions.

Autotextual mise en scène defines the dramatic text according to its uniqueness and historicity. It tries to understand the textual mechanisms and the structure of the plot according to an internal logic, with no reference to anything beyond the text to confirm or contradict it.

In this category, we find productions that try to reconstruct the historical context of the performance without opening up the text and the performance to the new *Social Context,* as well as productions hermetically sealed around a personal idea or thesis of the director and purportedly a total re-creation, with its own aesthetic principles.

This tendency, which was that of the "founder directors" (such as Gordon Craig or Adolph Appia), has been revived with a conception of mise en scène that claims to open up the text to a multiplicity of meanings, refusing to choose one particular reading, and thus maintaining the text in a state of undecidedness for the spectator (Peter Brook, Antoine Vitez).

Ideotextual mise en scène is the exact opposite. It is not so much the text itself that is staged as the political, social, and especially psychological subtext, almost as if the metatext—that is, the analysis of the work—sought to take the place of the actual text. The dramatic text is regarded as nothing more than a "dead weight," tolerated as an indeterminate signifying mass, placed indiscriminately either before or after the mise en scène. Staging a text therefore means being open to the outside world, even molding the textual object according to this world and the new circumstances of reception. The text loses its texture in such a mise en scène, having preconceived, extraneous knowledge and discourse added to it, taking its place in a global explanation of the world, a victim of what Michel Vinaver has called the "tyranny of ideologies." This kind of mise en scène takes over completely the role of mediator between the *Social Context* of the text produced in the past and the *Social Context* of the text received in the present by a given audience; it fulfills the "communication function" (Mukarovsky) for the work of art, making it possible for a new audience to read an old text. New meaning relationships in the scenic concretization are made manifest, thus reactivating the work-as-thing (i.e., the work as a signifier to be put into a concrete form).

Intertextual mise en scène provides the necessary mediation between autotextuality and ideological reference; it relativizes every new production as one possibility among others, placing it within a series of interpretations, every new solution trying to dissociate itself polemically from the others. Particularly as far as the French classical theatre is concerned, the mise en scène cannot help but declare its position in relation to past metatexts. This "interlucidity" applies to all compartments of the production: only by quoting can a stand be taken.

·   ·   ·

Taking a new structural definition of mise en scène as a starting point, we have been able to describe aspects of the mechanism of its reception and of the circuit of its textual and stage concretizations. The theory of fiction is the indispensable link in the production of meaning. It has not seemed feasible to extract from this theory any idea of what will happen to dramatic texts when they are read and produced once again; it is clearly impossible to foresee, for a given text, the range of potential mises en scène. The fault lies not with an impressionist theory but with the large number of variables, especially as far as the *Social Context* is concerned. The necessity of linking the textual and stage concretizations to the *Social Context* of the audience has become apparent. Concretization, fictionalization, and ideologization appear to be molds that cannot be used again for renewed readings.

The difficulty at present seems to be that of expressing in theoretical terms the manner in which a text experiments with several possible utterances. Utterance and rhythm in performance are still inadequately defined, for it has only just been realized that these are not restricted to gestural and visual changes but are germane to the whole mise en scène. It has now been understood and accepted that staging is not the mere physical uttering of a text with the appropriate intonation so that all can grasp the correct meaning; it is creating contexts of utterance in which the exchanges between verbal and nonverbal elements can take place. The utterance is always intended for an audience, with the result that mise en scène can no longer ignore the spectator and must even include him or her as the receptive pole in a circuit between the mise en scène produced by artists and the hypotheses of the spectators, artistically involved themselves in the mise en scène.

Theatre—the dramatic text as well as the mise en scène—has become a performance text (i.e., a theatrical production and experience impregnated with theorization). Mise en scène is becoming the self-reflexive discourse of the work of art as well as the desire for theorization experienced by an audience for which the functioning of the work of art must, in the words of a modern dictum, no longer "hold any secrets."

The modern work of art, and in particular the theatrical mise en scène, does not exist until we have explicitly extracted the system, the performance text, the pleasure of deconstruction and the control of the whole stage operation. "The discreet charm of good stage control," such is the name of the practical-theoretical entertainment to which we treat ourselves when we go to see Roger Planchon's *Tartuffe,* Giorgo Strehler's *Lear,* or Antoine Vitez's *Hamlet.*

Who then would still dare speak of the "birth of the performance" from a text, when an all-powerful director holds artistic sway? The semiotician of mise en scène, faithful to structuralism, is surely not tempted to use that worn-out phrase ever again.

NOTES

1. See, for example, Roman Ingarden, *The Literary Work of Art,* trans. G. Grabowicz (Evanston, Ill.: Northwestern University Press, 1973) and Jan Mukarovsky (who developed the concept of concretization), *The Word and Verbal Art* [Selected Essays], ed. and trans. J. Burbank and P. Steiner (New Haven & London: Yale University Press, 1977).

2. Jan Mukarovsky, "Art as Semiotic Fact," in *Structure, Sign and Function* [*Selected Essays*], ed. and trans. J. Burbank and P. Steiner (New Haven and London: Yale University Press, 1978), 88.

3. See John Searle, "The Logical Status of Fictional Discourse," *New Literary History* 6 (1975): 319–32.

4. John Styan, *Drama, Stage and Audience The Dramatic Experience* (Cambridge: Cambridge University Press, 1975), p. 75.

5. See Patrice Pavis, "Production, Reception and the Social Context," in *On Referring in Literature,* ed. Anna Whiteside and Michael Issacharoff (Bloomington: Indiana University Press, 1987).

A Medieval Prescription for Performance: *Le Jeu d'Adam*

ROBIN F. JONES

In medieval religious art, the Word became form; in the theatre, however, the full mystery was realized and the Word became flesh. In terms adapted, albeit proleptically, from Goethe's concept of *Stirb und Werde,* the dynamics of the incarnation might be formulated as *Schreib und Werde,*—that is, as a circular process, which leads from God to Goethe, from St. John's "In the beginning was the Word" to Faust's obsession with action, "Im Anfang war die Tat," and back again. The sacred playscript is the written score for the dramatic representation of the Word: upon the stage, it is converted into a complex of interdependent visual and verbal signs; in the mind of the spectator, the performance is reconverted, for, if to understand is to name, it is there reconstituted as words. However, since sign systems are not mutually convertible, the performance cannot repeat the playscript, nor can words of understanding reproduce the performance.[1] The Word is not simply transubstantiated in transmission, therefore, but transformed. The purpose of this essay is to follow the alchemic process in a particular text, *Le Jeu d'Adam,* with an eye to twin prescriptions for performance: that which directs the incarnation of the Word upon the stage and that which channels the perception of dramatic representation.

A discussion of dramatic performance and reception that starts with the written word of the playscript lays itself open unavoidably to objection, by reason of the implied assumption of the intention of live, dramatic representation. This reflection makes of the *Adam* a most suitable case for treatment. Medieval literature was mediated.

The saint's life, the epic, the courtly romance of the early Middle Ages were all sung or read to their public. They took place. In a literate age, any play can become "armchair" drama and frequently does, through the simple act of private reading. In the twelfth century, however, the dramatic text, like any other, was accessible to its public uniquely through performance. It is in recognition of this condition of the medieval text that Paul Zumthor writes, in his *Essai de poétique médiévale:* "Pour nous modernes le théâtre est un art que seul un abus de langage permet de classer parmi les genres littéraires. La situation médiévale originelle était inverse: toute poésie participait plus ou moins à ce que nous nommons théâtre."[2]

The degree of resemblance between medieval theatre and other contemporary literary genres is variable, yet however close the resemblance becomes, the theatre retains its distinction, for although all works of the period take place, theatre alone takes space. As the word *theatre* itself implies, physical space is the *sine qua non* of all dramatic representation. The constraints it imposes, to quote Keir Elam, "remain the primary influence on perception and reception."[3] Guided by these considerations, it will be on this most fundamental of theatre elements, its systems and its coding, that I shall concentrate in examining the prescription for performance present in the *Adam*, both as text for production and play for reception.

Space in the drama is of two essential kinds: the shown and the described, or, as Michael Issacharoff puts it, the mimetic and the diegetic.[4] The diegetic is the space evoked verbally by the characters but not visually present to the audience. The mimetic, however, is that which is represented on stage. The set of the *Adam*, in keeping with the general tendency of medieval culture to crystallize thought in plastic forms, represents the Christian universe; beyond it there is nowhere to evoke. The notion of events occurring in diegetic space, in places not visually present to the audience, is consequently inapplicable.[5]

There are four levels of the text that furnish information on mimetic space; dialogue, stage directions, lections, and responds. Of these, it is the stage directions that provide the most detailed, as well as the most authoritative, not to say authoritarian, statement of what is required. In this connection, the Latin in which they are couched is significant, although its use for the rubrics in early medieval vernacular theatre is not in itself an extraordinary practice. It is generally recognized that reception is conditioned by expectations generated from prior experience. The experience that served as a matrix for the expectations of the reader or "read to" of medieval Europe was inititally derived from Latin texts. Latin was a learned language used for special communicative functions, liturgical, scholastic, administrative. In short, it was the written vehicle for the transmission of truth and authority. Cast in Latin, therefore, the stage directions of the *Adam* express in form and content their control over the vernacular dialogue. What is true of the medium is equally true of its preferred mood, the subjunctive, used with imperative force. God's *fiat lux* is hardly more authoritative, at least for the grammarian, than the "Constituatur paradisus loco eminenciori" with which the stage directions or, more appropriately, stage directives for the play begin.[6]

The detail of the stage directions of the *Adam* has been a subject of frequent commentary, but for all their wealth they do not yield without resistance a serviceable visualization of the staging of the play, that is, of mimetic space. The problem is at first difficult to conceptualize, for when Issacharoff's classification of didascalia is applied to the play, the functions, labeled by him *nominative, destinatrice, mélodique, locative,* and *scénographique,* would all seem to be represented in functional detail.[7] The *Adam*'s opening rubric may serve to illustrate the point:

Constituatur paradisus loco eminenciori; circumponantur cortine et panni serici, ea altitudine, ut persone, que in paradiso erunt, possint videri sursum ad humeros; serantur odoriferi flores et frondes; sint in eo diverse arbores et fructus in eis dependentes, ut amenissimus locus videatur. Tunc veniat salvator indutus dalmatica, et statuantur coram eo Adam [et] Eva. Adam indutus sit tunica rubea, Eva vero muliebri vestimento albo, peplo serico albo, et stent ambo coram figura; Adam tamen proprius, vultu composito, Eva vero parum demissiori; et sit ipse Adam bene instructus, quando respondere debeat, ne ad respondendum nimis sit velox aut nimis tardus. Nec solum ipse, sed omnes persone sic instruantur, ut composite loquantur et gestum faciant convenientem rei, de qua loquuntur; et, in rithmis nec sillabam addant nec demant, sed omnes firmiter pronuncient, et dicantur seriatim que dicenda sunt. Quicunque nominaverit paradisum, respiciat eum et manu demonstret. Tunc incipiat lectio.

The names of the actors, the place in which they are to speak, the manner of delivery, gestures, costume, are all given. What then can be missing? The essential point to be borne in mind here is that the

Adam requires a multiple set, composed of various stations, visible to the audience for the duration of the performance. To answer my question, it is the location and orientation of the several components of the set that have been found problematic, rather than the design of the individual stations. The difficulty can be identified as locative, to use the labels alluded to earlier, but only in the somewhat stretched and cumbersome sense of the place within which the place within which the word takes place is placed. In multiple-set theatre, the locative function is best complemented by the configurative. Recognition of the configurative as a separate function permits a clearer distinction to be drawn between the station as the place in which segments of the dramatic action are performed and the placing of the stations relative to one another, according to some overall design. Locatively, the station frames the speech act it houses and is in turn framed by the set of which it is part. Configuratively, the stations construct a design that, as I shall later show, informs the locative and invests it semantically.[8]

What are the principal stations required for a performance of the *Adam,* and how are they to be disposed? Excluding such stage properties as the stones on which Cain and Abel sacrifice to God and the *scammum* from which the prophets address their audience, an inventory based on the rubrics and references in the dialogue includes: (1) celestial paradise, represented by the church; (2) terrestrial paradise; (3) the world; (4) hell. Of these, terrestrial paradise and hell would appear to be authentic mansions, purposefully designed constructions, providing a closed space before, within, toward, and away from which dramatic action took place. That this is true of the former will be clear from the rubric already quoted; that it is equally true of the latter can be deduced from the less precise but sufficient portrayal provided obliquely in the course of the stage direction describing how Adam and Even are to be led away by demons:

> Tunc veniet diabolus, et tres vel quatuor diaboli cum eo, deferentes in manibus chatenas et vincula ferrea, quos ponent in colla Ade et Eve. Et quidam eos inpellent, alii eos trahent ad infernum; alii vero diaboli erunt iuxta infernum obviam venientibus, et magnum tripudium inter se facient de eorum perdicione; et singuli alii diaboli illos venientes monstrabunt, et eos suscipient et in infernum mittent; et in eo facient fumum magnum ex[s]urgere, et vociferabuntur inter se in inferno gaudentes, et collident caldaria et lebetes suos, ut exterius audiantur. Et, facta aliquan-

tula mora, exibunt diaboli discurentes per plateas; quidam vero rema-
nebunt in inferno.

(p. 29)

On the basis of the opening rubric, which contains the direction
that terrestrial paradise be constructed *loco eminenciori,* it has been
regularly concluded that this station was to be located on a higher
level than the other components of the set. Some have imagined plat-
forms, even lofty scaffolds, equipped with ladders; others have suggested as a possible site the terrace at the top of the steps with which,
for the nonce, early medieval church architecture is made to equip
the entrances to its places of divine worship.[9] Both suggestions for
elevating Eden invite objection; the one with ladders, it has been
noted, would have been awkward, not to say dangerous, with God,
indutus dalmatica, in full ceremonial robes, human beings similarly at-
tired, demons and the Devil clambering up and down frequently.[10] In
terms of the sacred semiotics governing medieval space, it would also
have been unconventional, for it would have had the effect of placing
God's creatures physically higher than their creator. The same objection can be raised against the alternative solution, which situates terrestrial paradise at the top of the church steps and therefore on the
same level as God. Furthermore, the latter location would have provided at best only the most cramped of quarters for a garden, fruit
trees, Adam and Eve, and a corner in which to hide from God. There
would have been no room left for observing the rubrics: "Adam et
Eva spacientur, honeste delectantes in paradiso" (p. 7). At worst, however, the steps solution would have provided no room at all, for in
England contemporary church architecture appears to have favored
porches more or less at ground level. This applies even to the Norman cathedrals, of which none is capable of elevating a Garden of
Eden much above two feet.[11]

If the suggested locations for Eden are dubious in the light of
medieval convention and unacceptable on purely practical grounds,
they are equally so for textual reasons. Grace Frank has pointed out
that consistently the verbs used to indicate onstage movement in the
Adam are *venire, ire, vadere, accedere, recedere, ingredi, regredi,* but not
descendere or *ascendere*[12]; it is a reasonable assumption, therefore, that
movement to or from Eden is on the level; if this is so, it follows that
the location of Eden would be made to stand out by distance and not

by height. The rubric in which God is directed to return to the church following the settlement of the Garden argues in favor of this conclusion. The text is as follows: "Tunc vadet figura ad ecclesiam" (p. 7). Willem Noomen has drawn attention to the fact that the verb *vadere* conveys the idea of considerable remove[13]; an appropriate translation of the rubric would thus be: "Then let the figure make his way to the church." As for the interpretation of *eminens*, it should be noted that high is neither the only nor the single most usual sense of the word; the extended meaning, "conspicuous, remarkable," is equally well attested. There is clearly sufficient cause on purely practical grounds for doubting the traditional view of the elevated location of terrestrial paradise. Framed by this doubt, and in the context of the other references to the use of space in the *Adam* and the codes governing the use of sacred space in the Middle Ages, the extended sense of *eminens* would seem to provide the sounder reading. Thus interpreted, the stage direction at issue would seem to indicate that the intended site for earthly paradise was not on scaffolds or up stairs, but simply standing out from the façade of the church—that is, conspicuous by virtue of being downstage.

The location of terrestrial paradise downstage, which the foregoing observations recommend, is only possible within the context of the frontal stage and consequently argues in favor of its use. The incorporation into the set of the architecturally fixed church porch naturally precludes the autonomous platform stage, but not necessarily a theatre-in-the-round configuration. Against a circular set, however, in which, like Arthur's knights, all stations on the round are equal, is the special prominence of terrestrial paradise.

The stage directions are virtually silent on the whereabouts of the world and of hell. It is nonetheless possible to deduce their location with the help of significant omissions and allusions to the performance space inscribed in the dialogue.[14] Expelled from terrestrial paradise, Adam and Eve find themselves immediately in the world, the following words of divine wrath ringing in their ears:

Ore issez hors de paradis,
Mal change avez fet de païs.
En terre vus ferez maison:
En paradis n'avez raison.

(p. 24, l.491–94)

The rubric following these words describes the physical attitude of grief to be struck by Adam and Eve and contains the direction to take up spade and hoe to till the ground; but there is no mention of movement, either to a special station or simply away from terrestrial Paradise. In view of the careful attention to these details elsewhere, it is a sound conjecture that the world was to be represented by the *platea,* the undifferentiated space around and between the fixed mansions.

Beyond the world and at some distance from terrestrial paradise is hell. The opposition of "here" for the world and "there" for hell, in relation to terrestrial paradise, is suggested in the concluding part of God's speech of expulsion:

> Despois qu'avrez gustee mort,
> En emfer irrez sanz deport.
> Ici avront les cors eissil,
> Les almes en emfern peril.

(p. 25, l.505–07)

Situated beyond the world, the remoteness of hell from terrestrial paradise implied by these words is corroborated in the rubric in which the Devil, following his second unsuccessful attempt at precipitating the Fall, is directed to go from Eden "usque ad portas inferni," that is, "all the way to the gates of Hell" (p. 11). In the same rubric, the Devil is asked to leave the company of his demons and to walk among the spectators; the implication is that hell is situated close to the audience and consequently, like terrestrial paradise, located down stage.

In order of decreasing explicitness, references to the orientation of the stations, at all levels of the text, come last. Judging from the importance attached to such matters in medieval art and theatre, however, their placing was probably a matter of convention rather than one of no consequence. According to the sacred conventions of the period and, indeed, to an ageless tradition, right was regularly associated with good, left with evil. That the *Adam* follows convention is apparent from the rubric that describes the disposition of the stones upon which Cain and Abel are to sacrifice to God:

> Tunc ibunt ambo ad duos magnos lapides qui ad hoc erunt parati. Alter ab altero lapide erit remotus, ut cum aparuerit figura, sit lapis Abel ad dexteram eius, lapis vero Chaim ad sinistram. Abel offeret agnum et incensum, de quo faciet fumum ascendere. Chaym offeret maniplum

messis. Apparens itaque figura benedicet munera Abel et munera vero
Chaym despiciet.

(p. 33)

Since the areas on the right and left hands of God are, respectively,
places of honor and disfavor, the logical location for terrestrial paradise would be stage right and that of hell stage left.[15] In this connection, the physical nature of the performance area and the positioning
of the audience relative to it are obviously crucial. The space of the
autonomous platform stage and theatre-in-the-round was highly in-
formal; it abandoned to the spectator control over the orientation of
the components of the set; simply by changing position and moving
to the opposite side of the stage, or by turning 180°, the spectator
could transform stage right into stage left. The frontal stage, in contrast, relies upon a formal contract with the public, the members of
which are granted a single fixed perspective of the set.

With the play configured and oriented in the light of the foregoing
deliberations and performed on a frontal stage, the set of the *Adam*
would have been unalterably furnished with terrestrial paradise, the
world, and hell running in an unchangeable line from downstage
right to downstage left, at a modest distance from the church porch,
which signified heaven and also served as a backdrop.

In performance, the multiple set of the *Adam* has a dual mode of
existence and a dual mode of constraint in that the stations that com-
pose it may be regarded either as separate elements, or as combinations of these. At certain moments of the performance continuum,
the interaction of mimetic space with other channels singles out a
component of the set by overdetermination, distinguishing it as a location having special importance for the dramatic action. Although
the relevance of individual stations is emphasized in this way, all the
stations remain in full view for the duration of the performance,
whether foregrounded or not, and inevitably build a composite set
that, albeit discreetly, frames and gives meaning to the actions that
take place within it.

As might be expected, the "moments of polyphony" or overdetermination, which foreground the stations individually, coincide with
the major movements of the dramatic action—entry into Eden, expulsion, and death. In a performance of the *Adam*, three verbal channels would be heard on stage: the dialogue, the responsories, and the
lections. At the beginning of the play, when God establishes Adam

and Eve in Eden, in accordance with the rubric, "Tunc mittet eos in paradisum" (p. 5), two of these channels, the responsories and the dialogue, emphasize the event by duplicating what is apparent visually; to "Tulit ergo dominus hominem . . ." (p. 6) correspond the words spoken by God to his creatures: "Dedenz vus met" (1.86). The other stations in Adam and Eve's journey, the expulsion from paradise and the leading to hell, are similarly foregrounded verbally, the expulsion by God's imperative, "Ore issez hors de paradis" (l. 491), the passage to hell by Adam's announcement to Eve, "Menez serrums en emfer sanz entent" (l. 549), and by Eve's departing words, "Deus me rendra sa grace e sa mustrance, Nus gietera d'emfer par [sa] pussance" (ll. 589–90). The three stations of the couple's journey are further emphasized nonverbally. When cast out of paradise, Adam and Eve adopt an extreme posture, bowed down with sorrow: "quasi tristes et confusi, incurvati erunt solo tenus super talos suos" (p. 33). This contrasts with their previously upright attitude of innocent enjoyment in Eden, and their moderately bowed stance when they appear before God to confess: "Tunc ambo surgent stantes contra figuram, non tamen omnino erecti, sed ob verecundiam sui peccati aliquantulum curvati et multum tristes" (p. 28). In their vale of thorns, complete prostration follows the Devil's sowing of thistles: "Cum venient Adam et Eva ad culturam suam et viderint ortas spinas et tribulos, vehementi dolore percussi, prosternent se in terra, et residentes percucient pectora sua et femora sua, dolorem gestu fatentes" (p. 25). Fall and expulsion are mimed in their moral consequences, each stage and station marked by a progressively aggravated stooping, until finally the couple falls to the ground, beating their breasts and thighs in a show of violent grief.

A vestimentary system reinforces the verbal and the kinesic. On becoming aware of his sin, Adam, who is not naked, contrary to tradition, discards his *sollempnes vestes,* his formal red tunicle, and dons *vestes pauperes,* poor garments for the world, sewn with fig leaves, symbolic of his changed condition and imminent change of station. For the expulsion, God, previously *indutus dalmatica,* now appears *stolam habens,* stripped of the dalmatic and down to the stole. The point has been made by Lynette Muir that "the stole was (and is) the most important vestment, always worn for sacramental functions such as hearing confessions": its use here is consistent with the eminent "gravity of the situation and the priestly function of the wearer."[16]

The convergence upon mimetic space of the verbal, kinesic, and vestimentary channels, the principal means by which the play is conveyed to the spectator, sheds light on the system governing the use of space in the play and consequently on the function of space as a constraint governing perception and reception. The parts of the set through which Adam and Eve move on their journey from creation to death are at once foregrounded and differentiated by the interaction of systems in performance; entry into and departure from each area are verbally emphasized; each area is associated exclusively with specific elements of the kinesic and vestimentary codes. In a modern performance, it would be a simple matter to place a spotlight on the stations of the set in turn, as they are occupied; the moments of polyphony may be regarded as achieving the same effect; attention is drawn to the stations as a sequence of units at the expense of the set as a static arrangement of stations. This is not to dismiss the importance of the arrangement; the disposition of the stations, in line abreast and in order of occupation, makes of the sequential dynamic a processional principle. In his use of mimetic space, man in the *Adam* is obliged to move unidirectionally from stage right to stage left, from paradise, through the world to hell.

The second and third "acts" of the play—that is, the story of Cain and Abel and the *Ordo Prophetorum*—equally conform to the one-way principle of stage movement. Cain and Abel, eleven prophets, and an ass (Balaam's) appear on stage only to be led off by demons to the left. The processional principle is reinforced by the consecutive. Unlike the more or less contemporary *St. Resurreccion* and the later mystery plays, in which stations tended to remain inhabited for the duration of the performance, in the *Adam*, after strutting and fretting their brief moment on the *platea*, human beings, at least, must vacate the set that each new cross-stage movement may begin. The rubrics insist, for example, that the prophets be kept in a secret place, in the order in which they are to appear, be called onto the stage singly to deliver their prophecy, and be led away leftward, before the next prophet appears: "Tunc erunt parati prophete in loco secreto singuli, sicut eis convenit" (p. 37). In spite of Konigson, therefore, who, in *L'espace théâtral médiéval*, rejects the thesis formulated by Kernodle in *From Art to Theatre* and *Déroulement de la procession dans le temps*—namely, that a processional principle underlies medieval art and theatre—and in spite also of Konigson's gauntlet, that those who accept the processional solution are "épris de primitivisme," the *Adam* argues the presence, at the very beginning of medieval vernacular theatre, of a dominant processional dynamic.[17]

In contrast to the processional and consecutive principles that order all human existence after the Fall and direct motion through mimetic space, divines and devils move freely backward and forward along their respective axes of power: south/east and north/south for God and east/west and north/west for the Devil. God uses the southeast axis to travel between heaven (upstage center) and his tenants in paradise (downstage right). To receive Cain's and Abel's sacrifices, God moves downstage center along the northern line. The Devil uses the east/west axis to travel between hell (downstage left) and paradise, to sow tares in Adam's vale of tears and to lead all men away, west of Eden and out of the world. When he sallies forth into the audience to sow terror, the Devil follows a northwesterly route.

Beyond their material meanings of church porch, draped enclosure, churchyard, gates, and engines for making clatter and steam, the components of the set and the axial and oppositionary combinations into which they enter signify, independently of language, by reason of the overall configuration in which they are united: the form of the set makes sense of itself and of the secondary forms brought into the play in the course of the performance. This is so by reason of the connection existing between the geography of the set and medieval cosmography. In contemporary religious thought and in theatre, as Konigson has shown, right and left were the established doublets for East and West, which were in turn the universally accepted cardinal locations assigned by medieval cosmology to paradise and hell. Since right and left coincide with paradise and hell in the *Adam*, by reason of the fixed perspective imposed by the frontal stage, the configuration of the set finds itself linked by orientation and convention with the cardinal points of the compass. There is modest textual encouragement to make this connection in the rubric that instructs Abel, about to die, to genuflect to the East: "Tunc Abel flectet genua ad orientem" (p. 36). To observe the convention to which Abel here nods is to link the full complement of axes and oppositions contributed by the topography of the set in performance topologically to the four cardinal points. This connection of the compass and the stage has the effect of coding the forms of the latter with the values with which medieval Christendom, in particular church architecture, had invested the points of the former. The South regularly connoted the Word, divine law and authority, the North dark, cold and death, the East Jerusalem, paradise and bliss, the West hell, torment, but also redemption.[18] Significantly, the play concludes with the prophecy of Nebuchadnezzar, who foretells the presence of the Son of God with the faithful in the fiery furnace.

Clearly, the ideal performance site for the play would have been before the north wall of the church. Mimetic space would then simply have duplicated that of the church, reinforcing thereby the cardinal connection. Furthermore, the human journey from stage right to stage left, that is from East to West, would have been tied to the movement of the sun, to cosmic death and renewal, *Stirb und Werde*. The ideal performance time, one surmises, would have been the late afternoon.

Infused with meaning beyond its material sense, mimetic space serves as a low-level means of controlling perception by tacit commentary. The divinity of the *Figura* representing God is ensured by the fact that he enters and leaves the stage from the South. It is not clear from the rubrics whether the Devil is costumed as elegant tempter or as the feathered grotesque. Whatever his garb and kinship, his blandishments of Eve are beguiling and his offer of advancement convincing—but not for the audience, for whom the spell is broken and all illusion dispelled by the fact that the Devil makes his approach from the West. The "empty space" of the stations to be occupied as the play progresses maintains a dialectic with the action in progress, either confirming it or undermining it, but in either case providing the audience with a point of view for its evaluation. As Adam in paradise earnestly pledges to keep God's ordinance, affirming that it would be right to cast him forth into the world to die, should he but eat the apple, the earth and the tools to cultivate it await him down stage center, metonymically announcing his fall. Similarly, as Adam warns Eve that the Devil's tares are but the beginning of their tears, hell downstage left clatters and smokes in confirmation of the point.

In performance, the meanings inscribed by convention on the set of the *Adam* are confirmed, extended, and transformed by language. The process is at work in the extensive application of feudal terminology and formulas to the relationship between God and man.[19] Thus coded, the ultimate authority of Christian dogma becomes a vehicle for the reinforcement of the prevailing social institution. Be this as it may, the combination of these meanings into words of understanding is the job not of semantic potential but of constraint, exercised in performance by an arabesque of systems that guide and control the audience's pursuit of meaning, channeling it through a filigreed network of lines of interest. An essential thread in this interlace, space inevitably contributes to the reformulation of the originating word in reception.

In terms of movement alone, the dynamics of the *Adam* might be resumed as the conflict between inertia and motion, with man as the disputed object. God offers Adam eternal residence in the Garden of Eden in exchange for his unswerving obedience:

> Tot tens vivras, tant i ad bon estage:
> N'i porra ja changier li toen eage.
> Mort n'i crendras, ne te ferra damage.
> Ne voil qu'en isses, ici feras manage.

(ll.97–100)

The Devil's goal is to tear Adam and Eve from their rest in life and to set in motion their irreversible journey through the world to death.

In terms of space and movement, the play might be resumed as the opposition of the axial and the processional, of freedom to move up and down the relevant axes and the constraint to move unidirectionally 'out of play'.

In terms of the three basic spatial modalities in operation in performance—the architectural, the scenic, and the personal—the performance might be expressed as a war of constellations, of set groups or groups of sets, the one divine, joined by the south/east, north/south axes, and the other diabolical, joined by the east/west and north/east axes. Himself contested by good and evil, man is logically the body common to both. Linked by man, the components of the set, the twin constellations, form a whole divided against itself, a model signifying both the Christian universe and the Christian condition, the frame for and the prediction and determinant of the course of the dramatic action and its referent. Processionally constrained, there is no east of Eden for Adam, only west of hell, a round trip (it is hoped), leading to redemption. As a final word in this spatial recuperation of the word, it might be said, inspired by the religious and feudal resonances of the play, that the Devil tempts Eve not with an apple but with an axis, for what he in fact offers to her is nothing short of upward mobility through the ranks to the status of the ruling class:

Primes le prend e Adam done.
Del ciel avrez sempres corone,
Al greator serrez pareil
Ne vus purra celer conseil;
Puis que del fruit avrez mangié,
Sempres vus iert le cuer changié;
O Deu serrez [vus], sanz faillance,
D'egal bonté, d'egal puissance.
Guste del fruit.

(ll.263–71)

NOTES

1. See Emile Benveniste, *Problèmes de linguistique générale*, II (Paris: Gallimard, 1974), 53.

2. Paul Zumthor, *Essai de poétique médiévale* (Paris: Editions du Seuil, 1972), 431.

3. Keir Elam, *The Semiotics of Theatre and Drama* (New York and London: Methuen, 1980), 56.

4. Michael Issacharoff, "Space and Reference in Drama," *Poetics Today* 2, no. 3 (1981): 215.

5. See Elie Konigson, *L'espace théâtral médiéval* (Paris: CNRS, 1975) 290.

6. *Le Mystère d'Adam: an Anglo-Norman Drama of the Twelfth Century*, ed. Paul Studer, 5th ed. (Manchester: Manchester University Press, 1967), 1. All subsequent references to the text of the *Adam* are to this edition and appear in the text of the essay.

7. Michael Issacharoff, "Texte théâtral et didascalecture," *MLN* 96, no. 4 (1981): 818–21.

8. In *L'espace théâtral médiéval*, Konigson provides a survey of configurations characteristic of multiple-set theatre in the Middle Ages, 113–204.

9. The principal partisans of the scaffolding theory are Marius Sepet, *Le Drame chrétien au moyen âge* (Genève: Slatkine Reprints, 1975), 121–28; Karl Grass, ed., *Das Adamspiel, Anglo-normannisches Mysterium des XII Jahrhunderts*, 3rd rev. ed. (Halle [Saale]: M. Niemeyer, 1928) XXIII–XXV; Paul Studer, *Le Mystère d'Adam XXIV–XXVI* Gustave Cohen, *Histoire de la mise en scène dans le théâtre religieux du Moyen Age*, rev. ed. (Paris: Champion, 1926), 51–62. Exponents of the steps theory are Grace Frank, "The Genesis and Staging of the *Jeu d'Adam*," *PMLA* 59 (1944): 7–17; Michel Mathieu, "La mise en scène du *Mystère d'Adam*," *Marche Romane* 16 no. 2 (1966): 47–56.

10. See Frank, "The Genesis and Staging of the *Jeu d'Adam*," 12.

11. See Wolfgang Greisenegger, "Religiöses Schauspiel als politisches Instrument: Beobachtungen am altfranzösischen Adamspiel," *Maske und Ko-*

1 1 4

thurn 21 (1975): 9, n. 25; Bruce McConachie, "The Staging of the *Mystère d'Adam*," *Theatre Survey* 20 no. 1 (1979): 31.

12. Frank, "The Genesis and Staging of the *Jeu d'Adam*," 13–14.

13. Willem Noomen, "Le *Jeu d'Adam:* Etude descriptive et analytique," *Romania* 89 (1968): 191.

14. See McConachie, "The Staging of the *Mystère d'Adam*," 27. In spite of his attention to the evidence provided by the dialogue, McConachie clings to the traditional interpretation of in loco eminenciori and inexplicably assumes that earthly paradise must be immediately in front of the church.

15. See McConachie, "The Staging of the *Mystère d'Adam*," 32.

16. Lynette R. Muir, *Liturgy and Drama in the Anglo-Norman Adam* (Oxford: Blackwell, 1973), 38.

17. Konigson, *L'espace théâtral médiéval*, 275.

18. Ibid., 281–83.

19. See in particular Wendy Morgan, "'Who Was Then the Gentleman?':
Social, Historical, and Linguistic Codes in the *Mystère d'Adam*," *Studies in Philology* 79 (1982): 101–21.

Performance Orientations
in Ritual Theatre

RICHARD SCHECHNER

To speak of performance spaces is also to speak of performance rhythmicity and function—not only what spaces are used, but also for how long and in what ways. And it is not always true that space follows function, that a particular arrangement of a performance space is the way it is because of the way it is used. Certain shrines arise around special places: place comes first and around it precipitate definite kinds of performances. Noh drama may be considered, among other things, a theatre of marking special places. To speak of performance spaces is also to speak of rhythmicity: the alternation between activity and inactivity, sound and silence, fullness and emptiness. Table 1 compares various performances with regard to genre, space, and time in several cultures. I find almost no limits to what a performance may be, where it may take place, how long it takes to complete, what its functions are. There are private performances for no audiences, or audiences of one; there are performances with a live audience of more than a hundred thousand, and a media audience of many millions. There are performances that take place secretly, in remote places closed off from public view; and there are performances that aggressively try to reach as many people as possible, employing every available means of publicity and broadcasting. There are performances closely identified with specific places, so closely linked that a performance elsewhere is impossible; and there are performances that cannot be said to belong to any place.

The variety of performances is so great that it may not be helpful to generalize. I will concentrate my remarks on Ramlila of Ramnagar, a thirty-one-day cycle play of north India that tells the story of Rama's great war against the demon king, Ravana, and on Yaqui Easter, as celebrated in New Pascua, Arizona. The Yaqui passion play begins at Lent and ends on Easter Sunday; Holy Week, and especially Wednesday through Saturday, are climactic. Finally, I shall survey some experiments with performance space made by American theatre artists in the 1960s and 1970s.

I have described Ramlila in detail elsewhere.[1] Ramlila is a cycle play lasting ten to thirty-one days, performed outdoors in the Hindi-speaking region of North India. Its season is around the Dashahara holiday in September to October. Dashahara is Durga Puja in Bengali-speaking India—a very important day. Ramlila is based on Tulsidas's late sixteenth-century epic poem, *Ramcaritmanas,* a Hindi version of Valmiki's Sanskrit *Ramayana;* the Sanskrit's image is there in Tulsidas's Hindi, which stands in relation to the Valmiki as the King James version of the Bible stands in relation to the Hebrew and Aramaic. Then there are the *samvads,* the spoken dialogues written in the nineteenth century but revised as recently as 1927. Finally, there are the *bhajans* and *kirtans,* devotional songs sung by ordinary people in the audience as well as by holy men, *sadhus.* These songs are sung not only during the breaks in the performance and after the performance each night but also on the many boats crossing the Ganga River back from Ramnagar to Varanasi. Not only do the words of the various texts convey meaning, their very rhythms and tunes are important. Some of these melodies mean devotion, some ecstasy, some patriotism. Gandhi took one Ramlila song and made it a theme song of his struggle against the British. Although thousands of Ramlilas are performed, of varying complexity and duration, I have studied only one carefully: that of Ramnagar, acknowledged throughout India as the fullest, most theatrically sophisticated, and holiest of them all.

Ramnagar is across the Ganga River from Varanasi, also called Banaras, one of the most sacred cities in India. As a result of the patronage of the maharaja of Banaras, who lives in Ramnagar, this Ramlila draws the largest audiences of any. The subject matter of Ramlila is vast, touching themes of *Bhakti* (devotional worship), pilgrimage, reincarnation, nationalism, theatre, relationship between performer and role being performed, kingship, poetry, the secular government, and patronage. Here I will deal only with the space of the performance.

Table 1. Time/Space/Event Chart

	Aesthetic theatre	Sacred ritual	Secular ritual	Sports	Social drama	Minutes or less	Hours
Private and restricted	Theatre on Chekhov Street[a]	Initiation rites	Executions in U.S.A.	Sports played at home	Election of Pope	Execution	Theatre on Chekhov Stre
Private but open	Happenings and performance Art	Bar mitzvah	Ph.D. orals	Sandlot baseball	Murder trial	Puja at Hindu temple	Happenings, ballgames, etc
Local	Ordinary theatre and dance	Teyyam	Macy's Thanksgiving Parade	Big league baseball	Turnerian social drama	Stuart Sherman[c] street spectacle	ordinary theatre & dance
General	National network TV drama	Pilgrimage	Inauguration of U.S. President	Olympics	Hostage crisis; wars	TV commercials	Feature films
Sacred space	B& P in St. John the Divine	Religious events; Aborigine landscape	Town meeting in church	Aztec ballgame	Church where Pope is elected	Puja; eucharist	Ordinary church service
Secular space	Ordinary theatre & dance	Jewish circumcision; home wedding	Macy's Parade; Olympics	Playing fields	Town square; legislative hall	Stuart Sherman; Jewish circumcision	Ordinary theatre & dance
Found space	Rooftops, beaches, streets, galleries	Sacred trees, rocks, rivers	Parade routes	Sandlot ball	Wars; U.S. embassy during hostage crisis	Some happenings	Parades; some happenings
Transformed space	Stage set; environmental theatre	Churches; RL environments	Courtroom; execution chamber	Stadiums	Courtroom; throne-room	Execution	Orindary theatre & dance
Indoor space	Theatres	Churches, temples	Courtroom; execution chamber	Fieldhouses[h]	Courtroom; legislative hall	Some happenings; execution	Ordinary theatre & dance
Outdoor space	Greek or Elizabethan theatre	Aborigine initiation grounds	Parade route; U.S. inauguration	Stadiums	Tiwi "duel"[j]	Stuart Sherman	Greek or Elizabethan theatr
Single space	Ordinary theatre & dance	Church service	Courtroom	Stadiums, fieldhouses	Courtroom; legislative hall	Execution	Ordinary theatre & dance
Multispace	Many happenings; environmental theatre	Pilgrimage	Parades	Marathon running; Olympics	Hostage crisis	Some happenings; some guerrilla theatre	Some happenings

Examples are listed anecdotally. That is, many more examples could be given for almost every category. At this level, what is shown is the great diversity of performative events in terms of genre and use of time and space, and the interrelatedness of events, time, and space.

The chart can be read as a grid. For example, a Ph.D. oral examination is an example of "private but open" secular ritual; a town meeting held in a church is an example of a "secular ritual" taking place in a "sacred space"; the Macy's Thanksgiving Day Parade is a "calendrical-cyclical" event taking place in "found space," and so on. All items can be located according to three axes: event, time, space.

Not all items are so explained, but they can be. And some items, obviously, occur in more than one category. So, Ramlila is "multitime: segmented" plus "calendrical-cyclical" plus "symbolic time" plus "Days" in duration. But Ramlila is not so easy to locate in terms of whether or not it is "aesthetic theatre" or "sacred ritual" or "social drama." It is all of these, and at some moments more one than the others. Thus the chart's weakness: it categorizes, whereas many performances transform from one category to another or slip across categorical boundaries. Still, I have found making the chart helpful in organizing my thinking about performances, and I hope that it will be of use to others.

[a]The Theatre on Chekhov Street is one of several in Moscow operating privately outside the control of censorship. A description of it, and other private performances, is found in TDR 23, no. 4 (1979). Private restricted performances are common in places where public free expression is limited; they are also the mark of certain kinds of rituals that can be attended by certain people only.

[b]Sam Hsieh is a performance artist who specializes in "one year performances." According to Barry Kahn [Live 6/7 (1982): 40–42]: "On 30 September 1978, Sam Hsieh began a year of solitary confinement inside an 11′–6″ × 9′ × 8′ cell which he built within his studio. 'I shall not converse, read, write, listen to the radio or watch television until I unseal myself.' A friend, Cheng Wei Kwang, took charge of his food, clothing, and waste. At 5:00 p.m. on 11 April 1980, Sam Hsieh punched in on a standard industrial time clock he had installed in his studio, an act which he repeated every hour on the hour until 6:00 p.m. on 11 April 1981. On Saturday 26 September 1981, Sam Hsieh began his third one year performance: 'I shall stay outdoors for one year, never go inside. I shall not go in to [sic] a building, subway, train, car, airplane, ship, cave, tent. I shall have a sleeping bag,' his statement said." During his one year performances Hsieh allows the public to view him at certain times. For the outdoor performance anyone who knows who he is can watch him.

[c]Stuart Sherman stages "spectacles" on street corners, in theatre lobbies, in various other places not usually thought of as performance spaces. His spectacles are theatrically modest: a small table, an assembly of props all of which can fit in an attaché case, no dialogue; a total elapsed time of less than thirty minutes. As he became more successful, Sherman began inside theatres, on stage, in more orthodox ways.

[d]The Orokolo of Papua-New Guinea used to perform a cycle play that took years to complete. It is described by F. E. Williams in The Drama of the Orokolo (London: Oxford University Press, 1940), and also discussed extensively by me in "Actuals: A Look into Performance Theory" in Essays on Performance Theory (New York: Drama Book Specialists, 1977). Extended performances—

118

Table 1. (*continued*)

Days	Months or more	Single time, once only	Repeated	Multitime segmented	Calendrical cyclical	Event generated time	Symbolic time
Election of Pope	Some initiations	Execution	Theatre on Chekhov Street	Election of Pope	Some Aborigine performances	Election of Pope	Theatre on Chekhov Street
Some happenings	Sam Hsieh "Yearlong" performance[b]	Bar mitzvah		Some happenings	Puja at Hindu temple	Some happenings; sandlot baseball	Some happenings
Ramlila; Yaqui Easter	Orokolo cycle[d]	Some happenings	Ordinary theatre & dance	Ramlila; Yaqui Easter	Ramlila; Macy's Parade	Big-league ball	Ordinary theatre & dance
Olympics	TV soap operas	Boxing title match	Feature films	Olympics	Olympics; World Series	World Series	Feature films
Election of Pope; Aborigine ceremonies	Pilgrimage	Bar mitzvah		Yaqui Easter; Ramlila	Yaqui Easter; Ramlila		Ramlila; Yaqui Easter
Wilson's *Ka Mountain*[e]	Hostage crisis	Wilson's *Ka Mountain*; hostage crisis	Ordinary theatre & dance	World Series; Olympics	World Series; Olympics	Baseball	Ordinary theatre & dance
Wilson's *Ka Mountain*	Brook's theatre in Africa[f]	Many happenings and performance art		Aborigine ceremonies	Macy's Parade; Aborigine ceremonies	Sandlot baseball	Schechner's *Philoctetes* on beach[g]
Murder trial	Orokolo cycle; pilgrimage	Some happenings	Ordinary theatre & dance	Ramlila Yaqui Easter	Ramlila Yaqui Easter	World Series	Ordinary theatre & dance
Murder trial		Some happenings	Ordinary theatre & dance	Murder trial	Church services; folk Bugaku[i]	Indoor sports	Ordinary theatre & dance
Wilson's *Ka Mountain*	Orokolo cycle; pilgrimage	Some happenings	Elizabethan theatre	Ramlila; Yaqui Easter	Ramlila; Yaqui Easter	Baseball	Elizabethan theatre
Murder trial		Boxing title match	Ordinary theatre & dance	Murder trial	Folk Bugaku	Indoor sports	Ordinary theatre & dance
Olympics; Ramlila; Yaqui Easter	Orokolo cycle; hostage crisis	Hostage crisis	Ramlila; Yaqui Easter	Ramlila; Yaqui Easter	Ramlila; Yaqui Easter	World Series	Ramlila; Yaqui Easter

or connected cycles of performances—are not uncommon. A sports season can be thought of as a cycle of performances. Major league baseball is certainly this way—with several high points: opening game, "important series" near the end of the season, "traditional rivalries," playoffs, and the World Series.

[c]Robert Wilson staged a seven-day performance as part of the Shiraz Festival in 1972. It involved fifty persons and took 168 hours. It was staged on a mountian, and took the form of a kind of ascent or pilgrimage. *Ka Mountain* is described in an article by Ossia Trilling in *TDR* 175, no. 2 (1973): 33–47.

[f]From Decembjer 1972 through February 1973, Peter Brook and thirty actors, technicians, and support persons traveled by landrover through Africa from Algiers, across the Sahara, into Niger, Nigeria, Dahomey, Mali, and back to Algiers. During their trip they staged improvisations, exchanged theatrical (songs, dances, skits, techniques, etc.) items with Africans, and showed their own work. They played in many different situations. A uniting, and signaling, item was their "performance carpet." "We got out [of our vehicles]," said Brook, "unrolled our carpet, sat down, and an audience assembled in no time. And there was something incredible moving—because it was the total unknown, we didn't know what could be communicated, what couldn't. All we discovered after was that nothing had ever happened resembling this before on the market [at In-Salah, in Algeria]. Never had there been a strolling player or some little improvisation. There was no precedent for it. There was a feeling of simple and total attentiveness, total response and lightning appreciation, something that, perhaps in a second, changed every actor's sense of what a

relation with an audience could be." See "Brook's Africa: An Interview by Michael Gibson," in *TDR* 17 no. 3 (1973): 37–51.

[g]In 1960 I staged Sophocles' *Philoctetes* on the beach of Truro, Massachusetts (near Provincetown, where I was running a summer theatre). The audience had to walk over a mile of sand dunes to reach the place where the performance took place. Philoctetes himself roamed the dunes; Neoptolemus and Odysseus arrived by boat (we had launched them about a half-mile further down the beach). The Truro dunes really conveyed the sense of desert island that the Sophocles play asks for.

[h]Fieldhouses, as the name suggests, are indoor spaces that attempt to bring the outdoors inside. Even more out front in this intention are domed stadiums whose Astroturf looks like grass.

[i]In December 1979 I observed folk Bugaku in Northern Japan (Kazano City), at a Shinto Shrine. Peasants, wearing traditional masks, including a famous golden one said to possess great power, danced for about three hours on a makeshift square elevated stage—like a boxing ring without ropes—set up in the center of the interior of the shrine. It was said that this same performance is done each year, and dates back many hundreds of years.

[j]The Tiwi settle certain disputes by using a ritual duel staged in the main village square. The duel is described by C. W. M. Hart and Arnold R. Pilling in *The Tiwi of North Australia* (New York: Holt, Rinehart and Winston, 1966). Using their account I discuss the Tiwi duel in "Actuals." The Tiwi duel is a near-perfect example of Victor Turner's "social drama."

In Ramlila, the space is a complicated language of its own. To discuss it involves consideration of pilgrimage, processions, and the roles of the maharaja of Banaras, who sponsors Ramlila and oversees it personally and carefully, as king of the place. A king who is a king and is not a king simultaneously: since Indian independence in 1947, there have been no maharajas as such. Yet the maharaja of Banaras is always and universally referred to as the maharaja, treated as a maharaja, and even given government support for his projects, including Ramlila. He is provided with an honor guard of soldiers and a military marching band. Vibhuti Narain Singh thinks of himself as the maharaja, having been on the throne since 1937. To discuss Ramlila's space involves considerations of all these matters plus the actual mise-en-scène and its relationship to myth, to ancient and modern Indian history, and to local and national geography.

Ramnagar literally means "town of Rama." Fittingly named, for the town of Ramnagar is the actual setting for the enactment of Rama's deeds. During the first third of the nineteenth century, under the direct supervision of the maharajas of the time, numerous stage settings were built throughout the town in order to provide places for the various Ramlila performance events. Thus there is Ayodhya, the capital of Rama's kingdom; Janakpur, the home of Sita, his queen; Chitrakut, Rama's first residence in exile; Panchavati, the spot where Sita is kidnaped by Ravana, the ten-headed demon king of Lanka; and Lanka itself, Ravana's kingdom and site of the great battles between the armies of Ravana and Rama. In addition, there are the pathways and main streets of Ramnagar used for processions; and the main town square is used to depict the reunion of Rama, Sita, and Lakshman with their brothers when Rama's exile ends. And there is the outside and inside of the maharaja's fort, or palace, which becomes part of the drama in its final days.

The actual orientation of these spaces, as well as their relative positions in Ramnagar, is a more or less accurate model not only of India and Sri Lanka but also of Rama's movement through the countryside. The Ganga River makes a loop at Banaras (also called Varanasi and Kashi) so that the sun rises over the river, with Banaras on the west bank, Ramnagar on the east. Many cross the Ganga during Ramlila season by rowboat or ferry boat. (The flood-swollen river prevents the erection of a pontoon bridge used during the low-water season, and the permanent steel bridge is several miles downstream from Ramnagar.) As you approach Ramnagar by boat you see in the distance, under towering thunderheads, the great many-chambered fort of the maharaja. That fort anchors the Ramlila experience. Crossing the Ganga is something of a ritual crossing—into a liminal time/space. Returning to Varanasi by boat is a ritual reentering into the ordinary Varanasi world. These states of (sacred) being are relative, time-bound and layered or nested one in another. For both Ganga and Varanasi (when known by its ancient holy name of Kashi) are extremely sacred. Only during Ramlila, when, as people say, Rama walks the earth, is Ramnagar special. As on many ritual occasions, the normal order of things is inverted; holy Kashi and holy Ganga become, for this month only, the home base and entry gate (the literal limen) from which people come and return, and over and through which they cross, in order to enter temporarily the world and deeds of Rama. It is not by accident that Tulsidas entitled his Ramayana *Ramcaritmanas:* "The Holy lake of the deeds of Rama."

This crossing the Ganga to and from Ramlila helps orient the Ramlila environments in Ramnagar. Actually as well as ritually and mythopoetically, the fort and Rama's Ayodhya adjoining it are northwest of Lanka, which is far on the southeast edge of town. Janakpur, the birthplace of Sita, is to the north, and Chitrakut (also next to Rambagh, Rama's pleasure garden on the last night's *lila*) is to the northeast: a direction, I'm told, of good luck.

For most of the thirty-one days of Ramlila (each day's performance is called a *lila,* which means "play, sport, entertainment," but with a sacred connotation, "the gods at play"), Ramnagar is a living model of India, historical and mythic (see Figure 1). But on the last two to three days, Ramnagar becomes Ayodhya, Rama's capital. In one palace he is coronated; then he goes by elephant to his pleasure garden at Rambagh (near Chitrakut, and also near the place where the Ramlila begins, with Brahma granting Ravana the boons that allow the demon king to upset the balance of the world); finally, Rama and his family are carried in stately procession to the maharaja's fort, where they are honored by a state banquet and worshiped as the gods they are. All of these spaces are realized literally: they exist in several narrative, temporal, and existential frames simultaneously, and their meanings radiate through their multiple actualities. Ramnagar does not stop being Ramnagar; tea is sold, traffic moves in the streets, even as Ramnagar becomes India, Lanka, and Ayodhya.

The action of Ramlila is both physical and narrative. That is, the actual movement of the characters is itself a decisive part of the story:

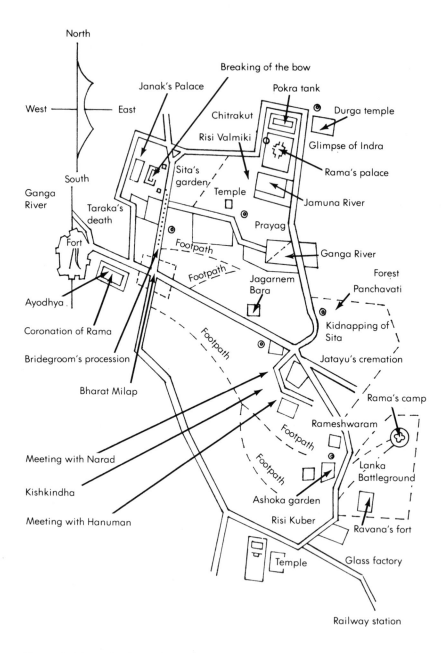

Figure 1. Map of Sri Ramlila ground, Ramnagar. From Richard Schechner, *Between Theater and Anthropology* (Philadelphia: University of Pennsylvania Press, 1985), 177. The map is based on a 1946 program distributed in Ramnagar, and is reasonably accurate even today in terms of location and scale.

122

movement has significance. The first night of the performance, when the gods implore Vishnu to incarnate himself as Rama, is performed around the *kshir sagar*, in front of an old and powerful Durga-Kali temple near Chitrakut and Rambagh, in the auspicious northeast. When Rama goes into exile, he crosses make-believe Ganga River, the holy river, as he heads from his capital at Ayodhya in the northwest, back toward the northeast. When Sita is kidnaped, Rama's army moves steadily to the southeast. This move parallels the actual historical movement through the India of the Sanskritic, Vedic culture, which the Aryan invaders of central Asia brought to India with them. Among the poems they made in India, merging Dravidian and other Indian traditions with their own, was the *Ramayana*. After days and nights of the climactic battles at Lanka, battles that have looked just about the same for 150 years, Rama defeats Ravana's armies and finally Ravana himself. A great celebration follows. Crowds of nearly one hundred thousand join in the dancing, singing, and feasting that occur between Ravana's surrender to Rama on the afternoon of the twenty-sixth *lila* and his spectacular cremation that night. Ravana's death and cremation always occur on Dashahara day: a time of great celebration throughout north India. Then on the next day Sita is liberated, her fidelity to Rama tested by an ordeal of fire, and Rama and his whole victorious party of family, monkeys and bears (plus whoever else can cram onto the great chariot) begin a slow procession from Lanka back to the center of Ramnagar, where in the twenty-eighth *lila* the Bharat Milap, the reunion of the four brothers, takes place. Rama and Lakshman's twelve-year exile is ended as they embrace their brothers Bharat and Satrughna. The Bharat Milap is staged in a boxing ring–like platform erected at the intersection of Ramnagar's two most important roads. From this point on, there follows, over the next three days, a series of splendid celebrations. These take place in Ayodhya, in Rambagh, in the fort, and, generally in a spirit of great festivity, throughout Ramnagar.

When the maharaja and his family honor Rama and his family, something very powerful theatrically and religiously creates a unique social, even political, situation. As mentioned, since 1947, when India became an independent, secular state, there has been, officially speaking, no maharaja of Banaras. All principalities were abolished, and a few years later, the privy purses were discontinued. Still everyone calls Vibhuti Narain Singh "Maharaja." Why? The answer in no small way is to be found in Ramlila. For the Ramlila season, especially during the performance of the *arati* temple service that concludes each evening's show, the *murtis*, images of the gods—boys playing Rama, Sita, Lakshman, Bharat, and Satrughna—are thought by many in the audience to actually be the gods they represent. It is a miracle parallel to Catholic transubstantiation. Thus, the presence of the *murtis* bestows on their patron and host a royalty that might by now be much diminished (as with some other former maharajas). But it's not quite that simple. It is more as though a symbiotic relationship and feedback tied up as well to the entire physical setting of Ramnagar, to the fact that for a month, in a whole town, Rama lives. The maharaja of Banaras is the only person with enough religious-traditional force to sponsor a great Ramlila. And the Ramlila in turn validates the maharaja's maharajadom. The climactic visit of mythic-theatrical Rama to the fort of the actual-theatrical maharaja is an intersection of ancient and modern, mythic and theatrical, extraordinary and ordinary time and space.

In Ramlila there are three kinds of movements in three spatial spheres—a situation parallel to the four spatial spheres of Yaqui Easter. The three movements are those of pilgrimage, those of the nightly performance, and those existing within a mythic narrative; and the three spatial spheres are of India, of Varanasi to Ramnagar and back, and of the Ramlila story. The three spheres are not concentric, nor does one replace or abolish any of the others. They all exist simultaneously as in a palimpsest.

The most far-flung sphere is that of those in the audience who consider the Ramnagar Ramlila a pilgrimage center. Many people take a month out of their lives to attend Ramlila, and some travel distances of more than one thousand miles to get to Ramnagar. More immediately, on a daily basis, many thousands of spectators cross the Ganga from Varanasi to attend Ramlila in Ramnagar. At the end of the night's performance they cross back, often singing *bhajans*, devotional songs, in honor of Rama, as they row back across the sacred river. To immerse oneself in Ganga is itself an act of purification. To cross the river daily to and from Ramlila is a sacred act. More than one boat capsizes each year, and some people drown. At a purely physical level of experience, this is clearly a bad thing, but at a spiritual level, as an expression of devotion within the context of Ramlila, some may regard it as a good thing.

The third sphere of movement, also immediate and actual, involves the processions and shifts of theatrical environment that constitute so much of Ramlila itself. At Ramnagar there are ten major shifts of locale. These shifts are precisely analogous to the Ramlila narrative. To attend Ramlila, therefore, is to participate with Rama in his adventures. Many thousands of spectators follow Rama into exile, weep when he weeps, cheer when he is victorious, celebrate when he returns to Ayodhya. Every time Rama speaks, many in the crowd shout (in Hindi): "Victory to King Rama!" Spectators bring him sweets and flowers, hold his feet in an act of submissive devotion. They cross the bridge of stones with Rama's army and invade Lanka; they throng around the triumphant Rama and his party on their return to Ayodhya. Not only do they treat Rama as a hero-god incarnate but also they devote themselves to Sita and Lakshman. Bharat and Satrughna are not so much in the story on a daily basis and therefore not the objects of so much attention. These movements and the crowd's devotion are not incidental or cosmetic. They are the core of the performance. They are the way people participate in the actual life of Rama. This participation is analogous to how medieval theatre in Europe moved its audience.

The environments of Ramlila are surprisingly detailed, constituting a correct model of the mythic narrative, even to being laid out in the correct directional orientation. Thus, the performance, like the narrative, moves from the northwest to the southeast and back again to the northwest. Throughout the month of Ramlila, each spectator is reminded that Rama's story takes place simultaneously in an actual and a mythic India, for the places in the narrative (Ayodhya, Lanka, Janakpur, Chitrakut, Panchavati) actually exist. And many spectators believe that by attending Ramlila they can visit these sacred places: to perform them in Ramlila is to bring them into existence for one month, just as the gods themselves, as *murtis*, exist for this same month. Thus, to move through Ramnagar is to move through India, not the India of today, but the India of Ramraj, the time when Rama ruled. This is an epoch not like today's debased Kali Yuga, but of an earlier, more perfect time. So the movement in space is also a movement in time; many who attend Ramlila feel they have been literally transported both spatially and temporally.

So do those who perform in Yaqui Easter. The performances I saw at New Pascua near Tucson, Arizona, though more modest theatrically, are very much like the Ramnagar Ramlila in terms of the use of space. At New Pascua, the organization of space contributes greatly to the bringing into theatrical existence of beings and forces that otherwise would remain unmanifest. (This process of making manifest the unmanifest is, I believe, one of the links connecting aesthetic and ritual theatre. It is also the area (of training and mise en scène) in which theatre specialists can exchange techniques with ritual specialists.) As with Ramlila, though not as extensively or with as many people, Easter is celebrated by Yaqui-speaking peoples in the United States and Mexico. My study of Yaqui Easter has just begun, and I will rely both on my own observations and the writings of Muriel Thayer Painter[2] and the magnificent studies of Edward H. Spicer,[3] who died in 1982.

The Yaqui situation is complicated by the fact that the ceremonies in New Pascua are versions of earlier observances performed in other places. This is doubly significant because the Yaqui placed a strong emphasis on place. The original eight Yaqui towns of Rio Yaqui in Mexico date from the early period of contact with the Jesuits in the seventeenth century. These towns, hundreds of miles from the Yaqui settlement in New Pascua, are both actual and mythical. They constitute an arena of Yaqui history as the Yaquis relate their history; they are also the place where the Yaqui say Christ walked during the three days between his crucifixion and resurrection. But before the eight towns, and surrounding them, as if they were islands, is the *huya aniya,* the wildlands, home of the Deer. As Spicer says:

> The *huya aniya* of the Yaquis is neither wholly separate from the Christian realm nor does it interpenetrate in a way comparable with that in the Christian-Maya synthesis. . . . Every ceremony devoted to a Christian supernatural required participation by ceremonialists whose power was associated with the *huya aniya.*[4]

Thus, the Easter passion play incorporates Deer and Pascola dancing, and a very dense interplay of these with two other kinds of performance figures: masked Chapayekas who pursue and crucify Christ and unmasked beribboned Matachin dancers who celebrate Christ's triumphant resurrection. This resurrection is marked by the throwing of flowers—flowers that actually drive back, disarm, and unmask the Chapayekas, who, defeated and transformed, burn their masks on a pyre piled up against one of the main crosses in the village square and then, unmasked, enter the church to gain the blessing of Christ.

This is parallel to the burning of the effigy Ravana on Dashahara night, near the end of the Ramlila. Fire is a way of purifying. It is also a way of soliciting and touching solar forces, sky forces, fire forces: heat and light, the sky itself. Ravana is more like a Christian Lucifer than an ordinary demon or devil. Ultimately Ravana is absorbed into Rama, forgiven and celebrated, as indeed the Chapayekas, who though they crucify Christ, are forgiven by him and accepted into his body (communion) when they burn their masks. They are blessed by the priest, they rejoin the Yaqui community. The symbolism is dense because it is supported by a dynamic system of conscious and unconscious oppositions and interpenetrations: countryside versus town, flowers versus masks, masked versus unmasked, Deer versus Pascola (ritual clown), Chapayekas versus Matachins, ancient musical instruments versus instruments introduced by the Spaniards, men versus women, adults versus children, pre-Colombian ceremony versus Jesuit-introduced Catholicism, and so on. To list these as oppositions reduces the elegance and complexity of their interrelatedness. I cannot here even begin to decipher this system. But I need to point out a few more cognitive, mythic, and ideological "movements" of the Yaqui that figure in their Easter performances, for these movements are recapitulated in the mise en scène itself.

The Jesuits entered Yaqui country in 1617. They were withdrawn in 1767. Much of what is celebrated today by the Yaqui took shape after the Jesuit withdrawal, when contact with Euro-Mexican power was occasional and often bloody. In the early twentieth century, a climax was reached in the relationship between Yaquis and Mexicans. The Mexican revolutionaries wanted to bring the Yaqui (and other Indian groups) into the Mexican nation, but on strictly Mexican terms. The struggles that followed, and continue to this day, resulted in at least two major dispersions of Yaqui. Many Yaqui were sent as forced laborers to the Yucatan. Others fled across the Rio Grande to Arizona, and some of these settled near Tucson. Thus, if the Jesuits introduced concentration—the establishment of the eight towns— the Mexicans forced diaspora. Most recently, in the 1960s and 1970s, as Tucson grew and encircled the Yaqui settlements there, a group of Yaquis led by Anselmo Valencia, who is both their political and religious leader, established New Pascua and won for it status as a federal Indian reservation. New Pascua is today the largest single settlement of Yaquis in the United States.

The land of New Pascua is regarded by the Yaquis as sacred territory. Thus, the recurrent pattern of Yaqui history from the first contact with the Europeans is one of concentration and dispersion,

Richard Schechner

settlement and diaspora, center and beyond (*huya aniya*). This pattern comprehends space as something significant in itself, and dynamic. This sense of significant movement is at the heart of Yaqui Easter.

During the performance, there are three visible and two implied spatial spheres. These are concentric, and there is much power in each of them, making for a complicated interrelation between the center, the midspace, and the beyond. The Easter ceremonies, though they can be studied from any number of perspectives, are extremely interesting as an unfolding relationship among these three spheres, for this relationship, theatrically speaking, can be discussed as a concrete mise en scène. The overall movement of the Easter performance is from the outside in, finally climaxing in the combat and absorption into the center of previously disruptive but plainly ancient and native, and therefore necessary, forces.

Figure 2 shows the arrangement of space for Easter in New Pascua. Beyond the stations of the cross (numbered 1 to 14) is the town of New Pascua, and beyond it the Anglo world of Arizona. The *huya aniya* is beyond the Anglo world. The food stalls are temporary structures that help delineate the sacred space that they surround and within which they are included. Inside the stalls is the interior outdoor space of the village and the church. The unnumbered cross immediately in front of the open church door marks the area where the inside of the church begins.

We in the West usually think that "inside" begins with a lintel, a doorway; the Yaqui think that the inside extends as far as the force of the church extends. So the inside begins outside: the church meets the rising sun. If the inside began inside the church, then the rising sun's light would not reach inside the church. The only way to have the sun in the church for a long time is to have the church extend to where there is no church, architecturally speaking. It is on this most sacred, most central area that the reconciliation between the Chapayekas and the rest of the town takes place, and where the Matachins dance their celebratory steps. There is another "open door," that of the ramada in the northeast of the square. In the ramada dance the Deer and Pascolas, a kind of sideshow. The significance of the Deer to Yaqui Easter is explained by Spicer thus:

> The Deer and the Pascola are essentially secular, but I am sure that the Deer Dancer has not always been so. Because they are not sacred, they may be danced throughout the Lenten period at household fiestas. Their meaning, despite being joyous like the Matachin dances, does not

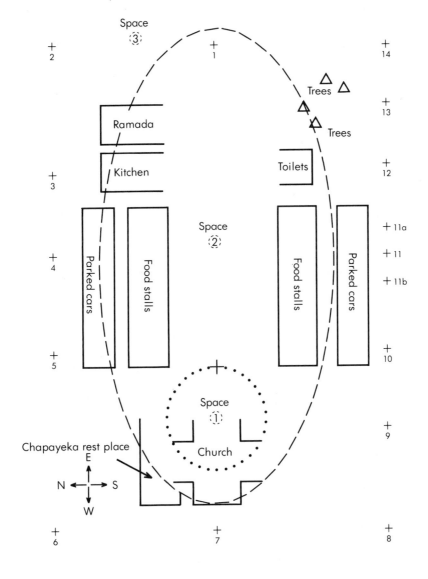

Space ⑤ is the *huya aniya*

Space ④ is the Anglo world of Arizona

Figure 2. The arrangement of space for Yaqui Easter

conflict with the Fariseo ritual meanings. It is just outside the realm of the sacred, and therefore not incompatible with the austerity and discipline of the Fariseo ceremonial season.[5]

When the Deer dances publicly, on Holy Saturday night as part of the Fiesta that celebrates Christ's victory (the victory of the "little angels"—young boys and girls whose thrown flower petals literally disarm and unmask the Chapayekas, both defeating and reconciling them), he does so in the Ramada: its open door being parallel to, not in conflict with, but, as Spicer points out, different from the open door of the church. And the Deer brings with him the space of *huya aniya,* and the flower world: the wild, the beyond.

Of all the spatial manipulations visible in the Yaqui forty-day passion play, let me concentrate on two only: the appearance and actions of the Chapayekas from Lent through Holy Saturday and the representation of the crucifixion itself on Good Friday. The first manifestation of the Chapayekas is the appearance of a single one who emerges from under the church altar on the first Friday of Lent:

> Slowly a figure emerges who is obviously out of place in the church. It looks around as though in puzzlement, but it is not easy to know what it thinks, for it says nothing and seems to be expressing uncertainty by knocking two painted sticks together tentatively. Moreover no facial expression is visible. The being wears a helmet of hide painted black, green, red, and white with two large loosely flapping ears and a slender pointed nose. It ignores the services in front of the altar where hymns and prayers preparatory for going around the Way of the Cross are in progress among the assembled townspeople. The Chapayeka goes up to the prayer leader and insolently cocks its head to look at him better, shuffles among the kneeling people, but when the name of the Blessed Virgin is mentioned begins to shiver and shake and then appears to wipe filth from its thighs with one of its sticks. In the midst of the solemn devotions, the Chapayeka suddenly shakes deer hoof rattles on a belt around his waist, momentarily drowning out the sacred chant. Turning his back on the altar, he trots among the people and out the door of the church.[6]

Then the Chapayeka joins the soldiers of Rome, whose camp is next to the church (see Figure 1). Accompanying the soldiers, the Chapayeka goes ahead of the faithful as they make their rounds of the Way of the Cross; the soldiers surround the faithful. Thus a pattern for Lent is set.

On the following Friday, two more Chapayekas enter town, this time from the northwest corner of the square. This entrance is farthest from station 11, the crucifixion cross, and not usually used to approach the church, the door of which opens eastward, toward the rising sun. One of the entering Chapayekas is the being from the previous Friday, and both Chapayekas seem a bit disoriented. Verging on the comical in appearance, they are also sinister and frightening. They carry their beating sticks, and the sound they make is a leitmotif of Yaqui Easter. It will be heard throughout Lent and mark the marching of the soldiers of Rome and the Chapayekas. The crucifixion itself—the hammering of imaginary nails with a wooden hammer into a cross at station 11—will echo this same sound of wood on wood. When the two Chapayekas see the church, they become agitated and uncertain. Then from somewhere else in town, two more Chapayekas appear. "Now elaborate gesturing takes place. It becomes evident that these beings communicate by using their sticks, employing various gestures and rhythmic beats."[7] The Chapayekas "demonstrate that they have come from somewhere to the north [a direction from which wild things come] and are very reluctant to stay in town and especially to go near the church."[8] The soldiers of Rome invite the Chapayekas to join them in their enterprise, the pursuit and crucifixion of Jesus. The Chapayekas express interest mostly in food and fiesta, but agree to join the soldiers, who promise the same. Thus the alliance against Jesus is made—an alliance that is parallel to the alliance Rama makes with Hanuman, the monkey general, and Jambuvan, the bear. The Chapayekas are in some way acculturated by the soldiers; even as they join against Jesus, they lay the groundwork for their eventual salvation.

But who are these Chapayekas who do not know what is going on? And why was the first one discovered inside the church they so evidently fear and avoid? I am not going to give an anthropological answer—that is, to use Spicer's considerable authority to assert that the Chapayekas are linked to Hopi and Zuni *kachinas* (which would surely place them to the north). I would rather stick to the theatrical evidence close at hand. By not knowing what is happening, the Chapayekas demonstrate their origins in a distant place both geographically and conceptually; they are literally out of touch with Jesus. By being discovered first in church, like a dog or even coyote that has strayed unknowingly into a holy place, the first Chapayeka demonstrates his innocence; the sophisticated soldiers of Rome must educate the Chapayekas to their evil purpose. But the discovery in church also fore-

Richard Schechner

shadows the resolution of the drama: it is a prediction acted out rather than spoken, as befits the mute Chapayekas; for on two more occasions the Chapayekas will enter the church. First, after they capture Jesus from Gethsemane, they will guard him in church, taking over that holy place and converting it entirely to their needs. Then on Holy Saturday, the Chapayekas will enter the church again, but this time as supplicants and devotees of Jesus. And, strictly speaking, they will enter not as Chapayekas at all, because their masks will have been discarded and burned. So the Chapayekas in church show a definite progression, passing from alien, unknowing, confused figures to sinister agents of the soldiers who crucify Jesus, and finally to transformed beings, townsmen who have shed their Chapayeka persona to become rededicated to Jesus. The "flower power" of the "little angels" literally unmasks and converts the Chapayekas into family men: for even as it is as lone males that they enter the town, it is as men with their families, their children and women, that they accept Jesus.

Each Friday during Lent more Chapayekas appear, until they number thirty-five or forty. "They are all outfitted according to a similar pattern, although some may wear old overcoats instead of blankets, and some are barefooted; others wear the traditional flat Yaqui sandals. But there is great variety in the masks. Each Chapayeka makes his own mask, and each is different."[9] In 1982, when I saw the Holy Week part of the Easter performance, I observed masks of many kinds: a goat, a sheep, a penis-nosed racoon, a Moor or Arab, a black-faced man in a top hat smoking a fat cigar, a pink-faced bald man, several "fantasy figures" of yellow, pink, black, and white, a yellow-faced man with Dracula teeth. All had the characteristic jug ears, and most had pointed thin noses.

It is apparent that the Chapayekas are under the influence of the soldiers of Rome, having agreed to help them, when they grow more and more intent on their one purposeful activity of tracking down Jesus. This is apparent with each new Friday procession, as they interfere with, almost jostle the faithful, pushing their sticks in front of them and turning over every tiny stone they come to, circle the processional groups, and silently taunt the Maestros [Yaqui priests] by dangling stuffed badgers and other animals over the prayer books. The Chapayekas in fact go all about the town, not only on Fridays but other days as well, spying on people and trying to catch children. People live in fear of possible punishments, and the tensions heighten as the Chapayekas make their presence increasingly felt.[10]

132

The Chapayekas are something like Namahage of Ota in Japan, or Halloween maskers in Euro-America: comic and sinister at once, originating in some other world (the north, the mountains, the dead) and making themselves visible and active in the world of human beings to which they really do not belong. But finally they are unmasked and revealed as loved relations and trusted neighbors: a fact everyone knew but, according to theatrical and religious convention, agreed to ignore. This willing suspension of disbelief is no trivial thing; it is the very key to worlds of subjunctivity, of "as if," to what Artaud called the "theatre and its double."

The processions around the Way of the Cross take Mary and Jesus and the faithful out into spatial sphere 3, away from the church, out of the plaza, out beyond the food stalls. It is dangerous out there. Going the Way of the Cross means losing sight of the church. The crucifixion crosses are set behind the stalls, near the toilets, in the far south and east, a direction (from the perspective of Rio Yaqui) from whence came both the Jesuits and the hated Mexicans, and the direction to which the Yaqui were deported at the end of the nineteenth century. The Yaqui Easter performance is not an uninterrupted tradition dating back centuries. It was stopped during the great diaspora: "For about twenty years, Yaquis did not carry out Easter Ceremonies anywhere. There was a hiatus in their continuity from about 1886 until 1906, when what has become the Old Pascua Ceremony was revived in Arizona. The Easter Ceremonies that we see today in Sonora are also revivals."[11] Thus when the Yaquis reinstituted their Easter performance they could consciously choose what to include, what to modify. The directional motifs are very particular: written in the geography of the performance is a model of Yaqui experience. Just as directors and movements have deep significance in Ramlila, so they do in Yaqui Easter.

On Thursday, the Chapayekas capture Jesus in Gethsemane and take him to the church, where they guard him throughout Thursday night of Holy Week. For the second time, now with a definite purpose, an evil purpose, the Chapayekas have penetrated the inner church itself.

There are actually two simultaneous processions around the Way of the Cross on Good Friday. One group, the largest, is led by a man who carries a large cross. This group proceeds in a counterclockwise direction, the "correct direction if the crucifixion is to take place at station 11. The other group, mostly women, bearing with them the effigies of the three Marys, move clockwise, but only for five stops, from station 1 back to station 11. Here there are three crosses, for three people are to be crucified, Jesus and the two thieves. The representation of the crucifixion itself, out of sight of the church, in the south to southeast in relation to the church, is done by having a man hit the wooden cross with a wooden mallet. There is no body, not even an effigy. But the sound of the wooden mallet striking the wooden cross is a version of the Chapayeka wooden stick music.

Once the crucifixion has taken place, the Chapayekas "swarm all through the church and out into the plaza. They uproot every cross of the Way, throwing each in the dust. They they play games and chase each other in a spirit of complete abandonment during the rest of Good Friday." By contrast, the rest of the town, the women especially, are solemn and in mourning for the crucified Jesus:

> There is a constant stream of mourners. One household has dedicated itself to provide a flower-bedecked bier in which to place the body of Christ. The decoration is elaborate, the highest effort of an entire family. The bier is blessed and borne to the church by a contingent of the Soldiers of Rome. The Adoration by the townspeople goes on all day and into the early night and creates a mood of deep sadness.[12]

The bier is inside the church. And in the bier is a small statue of Jesus. The feeling I got, in New Pascua in 1982, was of a combination bier-crèche. For the colors of the bier were bright, the effigy small, the feel of the cloth material like that of a crib.

The action of the passion play has now moved to the center of space 1: inside the church. The next morning, near noon, the soldiers of Rome and the Chapayekas storm the church. It is not clear exactly why: they have already won their victory. But they have not really occupied the church. Their camp is next to the church, and they have entered the church on several occasions, but it is still not their territory. They march in formation, clicking their sticks, and then they charge the church. But they are driven back by the little angels, who throw flowers at them. After three attempts, the Chapayekas are defeated, their masks are taken off and burned, and they enter the church as supplicants. The Matachin dancers begin their dancing, as do the Pascolas and Deer. At this point, the whole world, the space of the Way, the route of great agony, is ignored. At this moment, one can sense the theatrical and metaphysical function of the food stalls and parked cars: they block out the space of sphere 3 as the whole town celebrates in various ways in spheres 1 and 2: in the church, the ramada, the plaza, they eat, dance, socialize, and worship. And it is not easy, nor is it necessary, to make sharp distinctions among these activities.

What is clear from even this brief description of Ramlila and the Yaqui Easter is that these performances knit aesthetic, social, religious, and mythic themes together, and that the actual physical space and mise en scène of the performances are in important ways assertions of these themes. That is to say that although the Ramlila and Yaqui performances follow certain aesthetic conventions with regard to dance steps, costumes, dialogue delivery, and so on, in the matter of overall scenography—the use of the town as stage—a mythic-religious model has been constructed. In this large mise en scène, aesthetics is less important than the provision of an actual geography in which to act out important material that seems to find its most powerful form not as literature but as theatre. It is precisely this kind of meta-aesthetics, which goes beyond aesthetics, which contemporary Western theatre lacks.

Experimentalists have felt this lack and have, in their own ways, tried to remedy it. Again, many of these experiments over the past thirty years or so have taken the pathway of exploring new kinds of theatrical space. Experiments in environmental theatre, and in audience participation (even to the dissolution of the audience altogether by Jerzy Grotowski), have been major avenues of meta-aesthetics in Euro-American theatre.

Of course, at least since the Bauhaus, artists have designed "total theatres," but it was not until the 1960s that such ideas were translated in a large way into theatrical practice. Some of the theoretical basis for this is outlined in my 1968 article, "Six Axioms for Environmental Theatre." The first axiom is that "the theatrical event is a set of related transactions." This relocates theatre, distancing it from the enactment of a fixed literary text and setting in the performance space, between performers and spectators, events and space, production elements and texts (not necessarily written texts). The second axiom is that "all the space is used for performance; all the space is used for audience":

> Once one gives up fixed seating and the bifurcation of space, entirely new relationships are possible. Body contact can naturally occur between performers and audience; voice levels and acting intensities can be widely varied; a sense of shared experience can be engendered. Most important, each scene can create its own space, either contracting to a

central spot or a remote area or expanding to fill all available space. The action "breathes" and the audience itself becomes a major scenic element.[13]

What environmental theatre gives is a "global sense" of theatrical space rather than a "stage sense" of simulated space. Many of the theatrical experiments in Europe and America over the past twenty-five years have tried to use space in roughly the same way as it is used in Ramlila and Yaqui Easter. Experimenters wanted to make scenography/geography "speak," just as it speaks in Ramnagar and New Pascua—and not just stage settings, but whole spaces that included audiences and transformed them into participants. The difficulty is an ambivalence, even a hostility on the part of the Westernized, conventionally distanced audience toward such experiments. The ambivalence is rooted in the differences between social, aesthetic, political, and religious thought and action in Euro-American cultures. It is precisely this ambivalence and hostility that is missing in Ramlila and Yaqui Easter. There, certain figures, demons and Chapayekas, are permitted aggressive, obscene, and even sacrilegious acts; but these are played out, nested within the assurance of ultimate reconciliation and redemption. Ravana's final surrender to Rama, an exact parallel to the Chapayekas' redemption in Yaqui Easter, is to remove his mask and touch the feet of Rama. Ravana is defeated; the actor playing Ravana is redeemed.

I've come to the place where divergent societies and cultural values give rise to different kinds of theatre. Theatre experimenters in Europe and America, and in Asia and Africa as well, have tried to include their audiences by creating special spaces and ritual-aesthetic actions. Did they or will they suceed in diminishing the distance—actual, social, political, psychic, and ontological—between the performance, the performers, and the spectators?

NOTES

1. Richard Schechner, *Between Theater and Anthropology* (Philadelphia: University of Pennsylvania Press, 1985), 151–212.

2. Muriel Thayer Painter, *A Yaqui Easter* (Tucson: University of Arizona Press, 1971); *With Good Heart* (Tucson: University of Arizona Press, 1986).

3. Edward H. Spicer, *Pascua: A Yaqui Village in Arizona* (Tucson: University of Arizona Press, 1967); "The Context of the Yaqui Easter Ceremony," in *CORD Research Annual VI. New Dimensions in Dance Research: Anthropology and*

Dance—The American Indian, ed. Tamara Comstock (New York: Committee on Research in Dance, New York University, 1974); *The Yaquis: A Cultural History* (Tucson: University of Arizona Press, 1980).

4. Spicer, *The Yaquis,* 69–70.

5. Spicer, "Context," 322.

6. Spicer, *The Yaquis,* 76.

7. Ibid., 77.

8. Ibid.

9. Ibid., 78.

10. Ibid.

11. Spicer, "Context," 33.

12. Spicer, *The Yaquis,* 80.

13. Richard Schechner, "Six Axioms for Environmental Theatre," *The Drama Review* 12 (Spring 1968): 49.

Postscript or Pinch of Salt: Performance as Mediation or Deconstruction

MICHAEL ISSACHAROFF

All literary texts, whether or not they are playscripts, are mediated. Privately, if they are novels—the reader fleshes out, in the mind's eye, the pages read in the quiet of the study. Publicly, in the case of playscripts. Private mediation is no more than a limited form of concretization or actualization that breathes life into a novel, for the ordinary reader is not obliged to communicate the readerly experience. The latter may be only half-consciously realized, when readerly impressions remain unarticulated. The nonprofessional reader has no reason to justify his or her response or convince anyone either in speech or in print.

Though the activity is, perhaps, individual and isolated, the reader's experience is likely to have been the product of a mediatory process, influenced, say, by reviews, interviews in the media, and so forth. And thus, a form of articulated mediation occurs to the extent that the reader's response or horizon of expectation is a conditioned process.

In short, then, it is probably impossible for the reader to achieve a complete *tabula rasa* in his or her mind. If the reader has not been influenced by extraneous material about the text, he or she nevertheless is likely to read the novel, play, or poem through the mediation of the conventions to which it belongs. Necessarily, the reader's role is always to some degree intertextual—no literary work can be read in a complete vacuum.

Postscript

What characterizes the playscript is the two-way process of mediation that occurs. There is first the kind of mediation, comparable to the novel-reader's experience, when the producer and cast read the playscript. Their response, like that of the amateur reader of fiction, is partly conditioned by the conventions to which the particular play belongs, their knowledge of other plays, and so forth. The other side of the coin is the mediation that takes place through the performance itself, which mediates for the spectator. It need hardly be said that any production entails an interpretation. All worthwhile productions aim to do more than merely repeat what has been done by previous producers. A production thus programs an audience response, attempts to convince playgoers that Shakespeare's *Richard II*, for example, can be seen through the kabuki prism.

But contrary to the mode of private mediation, public mediation entails a collective effort. Channeling a playgoer's perception of a play requires a disciplined, concentrated focus that starts with the director but must be complemented by the cast and stage team. The audience, like the cast, must to some extent be brought to accept a single, if not a singular, vision of a given work.

The author of a playscript may attempt to achieve the channeling through didascalia—in a more or less authoritarian fashion; hence playscripts with abundant didascalia or even the extreme case of Beckett's *Act Without Words* (I or II), consisting exclusively of stage directions (and no dialogue). There are other possibilities at the playwright's disposal, including performance inscribed in the dialogue, which also may attempt to condition, thereby doing a simultaneous job of expression and mediation.

In short, then, the two modes of mediation—private and public—are closely related. Public mediation is, of course, the more complex of the two—in fact, a reduplication of the private process. But mediation is never neutral or passive. As we shall see, performance undermines the notion of the text as the repository of stable meaning. In short, it is in some ways comparable with deconstructionist strategies of text processing. The playscript is in no way "sacred"; performance is never merely a "translation" of it to the stage. To exist, it is contingent on performance. The director, as we have seen, is public mediator. His or her role is akin to that of the critic. Now, if we accept Hartman's point that criticism should not be subservient to literature,

teaching, criticizing and presenting the great texts of our culture are essential tasks [but] to insist on the importance of literature should not entail assigning to literary criticism only a service function. Criticism is part of the world of letters, and has its own mixed philosophical and literary reflective and figural strength.[1]

it becomes apparent that the traditional hierarchy that places text above performance is seriously undermined. The deconstructionist position with regard to literary criticism is radical. It attempts to grant a refurbished role to the critic. As Christopher Norris writes:

> there is no longer the sense of a primal authority attaching to the literary work and requiring that criticism keep its respectful distance. The autonomy of the text is actively invaded by a new and insubordinate style of commentary which puts in question all the traditional attributes of literary meaning.[2]

One could therefore argue that performance can be a mode of deconstruction; the director may, if he so chooses, borrow the hat of the deconstructionist critic.

Most of the essays in this volume implicitly exemplify stances close to deconstructionist, and specifically Derridean, strategies. Alter and Schechner, for example, privilege performance over regular scripted plays, thereby avoiding logocentric theatre repudiated by Artaud, that form of drama described as "theological" by Derrida in his reading of Artaud in *L'Ecriture et la différence*. The stage, Derrida argues, is theological as long as it is dominated by the Word, a primary logos, alien to the theatrical space that it governs from a distance.[3] The kind of performances described by Schechner and Alter succeed in eliminating the tyranny of the text.[4] The examples of "regular" drama studied by Styan, Whiteside, and Elam deliberately subvert the frame of the stage, which normally enforces the distinction between disengaged speech act and speech event in which the audience is actively involved. The critical consequences of the Pavis, Jones, and Issacharoff chapters are no less deconstructionist: Pavis in privileging the producer's potential freedom from textual constraint, Jones in true Artaud-Derridean fashion by foregrounding the primacy of the nonverbal channels and the way they shape meaning, Issacharoff by basing the cohesion of the playscript on a channel that in many instances may not be differentiated from the dialogue (as in Shakespeare) or that otherwise can be subverted (at some risk, to recall Alter) by the director—the stage directions.

Nevertheless, if these comments give the (mistaken) impression of an attempt to recuperate the essays, to undermine their apparently semiotic allegiance, I hasten to add that not only would that be a naive reading of this end note, but it would also be a misunderstanding of the semiotic framework of the essays, some of which explicitly valorize the contradictions implicit in the semiotic enterprise itself. Deconstruction, in any case, as Derrida (and many of his commentators) have pointed out, should in no way be seen to "cancel out" semiotics. As Derrida has argued, metaphysical presuppositions and critical motifs are not incompatible.[5] In deconstructing Saussure's binary construct (signifier/signified), for example, Derrida insisted, in *De la grammatologie,* that his enterprise, far from jettisoning Saussure's binary opposition, aimed to exploit its internal contradictions instead.[6]

But this is not the place to consider the many parallels to be made between performance and deconstruction, which could include, among others, *différance* (and its links with intertextuality, for example) and the status of meaning in the playscript. But it is worth examining briefly one issue central both to performance and speech-act theory as deconstructed by Derrida—the problem of citation or iterability. Austin, it will be recalled, in differentiating between performative and nonperformative utterances, maintained that repetition, as in the case of the actor speaking lines on stage, disengages what is said, which, he thought, thereby becomes "hollow" and "void."[7] In a rather neat critique of Austin,[8] Derrida counters that the so-called performative itself is contingent on conventionalized utterances—it too is necessarily "cited" or repeated. Derrida concludes from this that iterability (as in a signature, a ritualized utterance, and so forth) in no way precludes the possibility of successful performatives. In fact, the performative depends on the ritualized preexistence of a given utterance. The issue then, as Derrida points out, is not repetition versus the unique speech event, but the nature of repetition itself: "Rather than oppose citation or iteration to the non-iteration of an event one ought to construct a differential typology of forms of iteration, assuming that such a project is tenable and can result in an exhaustive program."[9]

Derrida's critique of Austin thus raises (for our purposes) a rather interesting problem: the status of stage utterances. Clearly what is said on stage is "cited"—in selecting and editing a playscript, the director is citing a text, which is in turn cited by the players.[10] Like a performative utterance in nonliterary situations, a performance of, say, a play by Shakespeare is contingent on the existence of a script by that author, recognized by an audience. The problem, then, is the status of Shakespeare's script in performance. Is it, as Austin would hold, a series of "hollow" utterances disengaged from reality, or could it have performative potential? That problem is even more complex than it first appears, since it entails another: the notion of (Shakespeare's) "text." The latter, too, can be deconstructed, given that a text, far from being an absolute entity, contains traces of texts that precede it. In other words, dramatic speech acts and intertextuality must necessarily be explored in tandem as performing texts, transcending barriers within the performance space and beyond. One of the implicit purposes of this book has been to eliminate (or deconstruct) another barrier—that between theatre and "mainstream" literary theory.

NOTES

1. Geoffrey Hartman, "Preface," in Harold Bloom [et al.], *Deconstruction and Criticism*, (New York: Continuum, 1979), vii.

2. Christopher Norris, *Deconstruction: Theory and Practice* (London and New York: Methuen, 1982), 24.

3. Jacques Derrida, *L'Ecriture et la différence* (Paris: Seuil, 1967), 345.

4. Echoing Artaud, Derrida argues that if the tyranny of the text can be overthrown, creativity in mise en scène becomes possible: "Délivrée du texte et du dieu-auteur, la mise en scène serait donc rendue à sa liberté créatrice et instauratrice. Le metteur en scène et les participants (qui ne seraient plus acteurs *ou* spectateurs) cesseraient d'être les instruments et les organes de la représentation." *L'Ecriture et la différence*, 348.

5. See, especially, Derrida, *Positions* (Paris: Minuit, 1972), 49–50.

6. "Bien entendu, il ne s'agit pas de rejeter ces notions [signifiant/signifié]: elles sont nécessaires, et aujourd'hui du moins, pour nous, plus rien n'est pensable sans elles." *De la grammatologie* (Paris: Minuit, 1967), 25.

7. J. L. Austin, *How To Do Things With Words* (Oxford: Clarendon Press, 1962). In a study of Austin's rhetoric, Christopher Norris shows how Austin frequently relies on examples from fictional discourse to illustrate his position and frequently subverts his own distinctions, at times adopting a quasi-deconstructionist stance. See *The Deconstructive Turn* (London and New York: Methuen, 1983), 59–84.

8. Jacques Derrida, "Signature Event Context," *Glyph* 1 (1977): 172–97. (See also John Searle's unconvincing rejoinder, "Reiterating the Differences (Reply to Derrida)," *Glyph* 1 (1977): 198–208, as well as Derrida's playful response: "Limited Inc. abc," *Glyph* 2 (1977): 162–254.

9. Derrida, "Signature Event Context," 192.

Postscript

10. On the general problem of citationality and intertextuality, see J. Hillis Miller, "The Critic as Host," in H. Bloom [et al.], *Deconstruction and Criticism*, 217–53. See also Michael Issacharoff, *Le Spectacle du discours* (Paris: José Corti, 1985), 41–65.

Bibliography

The following is a guide to further reading on the theory of the theatre. It is not intended to be exhaustive. Not included are studies on particular plays or dramatists or general theoretical works whose focus is not primarily the theatre. Complementary information (with examples of semiotic or other theoretical analyses of individual plays) will be found in Schmid and Van Kesteren, *Semiotics of Drama and Theatre*, 513–48.

Abel, L. *Metatheatre: A New View of Dramatic Form*. New York: Hill and Wang, 1963.

Alter, J. "Coding Dramatic Efficiency in Plays: From Text to Stage." *Semiotica* 28, no. 3–4 (1979): 247–57.

———. "From Text to Performance." *Poetics Today* 2, no. 3 (1981): 113–39.

———. "Performance and Performance. On the Margin of Theatre Semiotics." *Degrés* 30 (1982): d1–d14.

Arnott, J.; Chariau, J.; Huesmann, H.; Lawrenson, T.; Theobald, R., Eds. *Theatre Space. An Examination of the Interaction between Space, Technology, Performance and Society*. Munich: International Federation for Theatre Research, 1977.

Barry, J. *Dramatic Structure: The Shaping of Experience*. Berkeley: University of California Press, 1970.

Beckerman, B., "Acts of Truth and Wonder." *Maske und Kothurn: Internationale Beiträge zur Theaterwissenschaft* 29 (1983): 179–88.

Bettelini, G. "Appunti per una semiotica del teatro." In *Teatro e communicazione*, edited by G. Bettelini and M. de Marinis. Florence: Guaraldi, 1977, 9–32.

Blau, H. "Universals of Performance: or, Amortizing Play." *SubStance* 11–12 (1983): 140–61.

Bogatyrev, P. "Les signes du théâtre." *Poétique* 8 (1971): 517–30.

Bouissac, P. *La Mesure des gestes: Prolégomènes à la sémiotique gestuelle*. The Hague: Mouton, 1973.

Brook, P. *The Empty Space*. London: McGibbon & Kee, 1968.

Bibliography

Burns, E. *Theatricality: A Study of Convention in the Theatre and in Social Life.* London: Longman, 1978.

Canziani, R. *Il dramma e lo spettacolo.* Rome: Ateneo, 1984.

Carlson, M. "The Semiotics of Character Names in the Drama." *Semiotica* 44, no. 3–4 (1983): 283–96.

———. *Theories of the Theatre.* Ithaca: Cornell University Press, 1984.

Cascetta, A., ed. *I discorsi del teatro.* Milan: Vita e Pensiero, 1982.

Chambers, R. "Le Masque et le miroir: Vers une théorie relationnelle du théâtre." *Etudes littéraires* 13, no. 3 (1980): 397–412.

Corvin, M. "La redondance du signe dans le fonctionnement théâtral." *Degrés* 13 (1978): c–c23.

———. "La détermination des unités en sémiologie théâtrale." In *Regards sur la sémiologie contemporaine,* edited by L. Roux. Saint-Etienne: Université de Saint-Etienne, Centre Interdisciplinaire d'Etudes et de Recherches sur l'Expression Contemporaine, 1978.

Corvin, M., ed. *Sémiologie et théâtre [Organon 80],* 1980.

Cravetto, M. "Paradoxe théâtral: Jeu de miroir/jeu d'échec." *Littérature* 43 (1981): 75–88.

Degrés 13 (1978); 29, 30 (1982).

Deak, F. "Structuralism in Theatre: The Prague School Contribution." *The Drama Review* 20 (1976): 83–94.

Derrida, J. *L'Ecriture et la différence.* Paris: Seuil, 1967.

Dispositio 12 (1987), Special issue on semiotics of theatre.

Dodd, W. "Metalanguage and Character in Drama." *Lingua e stile* 14, no. 1 (1979): 135–50.

———. "Conversation, Dialogue and Exposition." *Strumenti Critici 44* (1981): 171–91.

Dodd, W. et al. *Interazione, dialogo, convenzioni.* Bologna: Cooperativa Libraria Universitaria Editrice, 1983.

Durand, R., ed. *La Relation théâtrale.* Lille: Presses Universitaires de Lille, 1980.

———. "Theatre/SIGNS/Performance: On Some Transformations of the Theatrical and the Theoretical." In *Innovation/Renovation: New Perspectives on the Humanities,* edited by I. and S. Hassan. Madison: University of Wisconsin Press, 1983.

Elam, K. "Language in the Theatre," *SubStance* 18–19 (1979): 139–62.

———. *Semiotics of Theatre and Drama.* London: Methuen, 1980.

Ertel, E. "Eléments pour une sémiologie du théâtre." *Travail Théâtral* 28–29 (1977): 121–50.

Etudes Littéraires 13, no. 3 (1980) (Théâtre et théâtralité. Essais d'études sémiotiques).

Féral, J.; Savona, J.; and Walker, E., eds. *Théâtralité, écriture et mise en scène.* Québec: Hurtebise, 1985.

Bibliography

Ferroni, G., ed. *La Semiotica e il doppio teatrale.* Naples: Liguori, 1981.

Finter, H. "Experimental Theatre and Semiology of Theatre: The Theatricalization of Voice." *Modern Drama* 26, no. 4 (1983): 501–17.

Fischer-Lichte, E. *Semiotik des Theaters: eine Einführung.* Tübingen: Narr, 1983.

Forestier, G. *Le Théâtre dans le théâtre sur la scène française du dix-septième siècle.* Geneva: Droz, 1981.

Francoeur, L. "Eléments pour une théâtrologie." *Semiotica* 31, no. 3–4 (1980): 245–59.

Fricke, H. "Semantics or Pragmatics of Fictionality: A Modest Proposal." *Poetics* 11, no. 4–6 (1982): 439–52.

Gale, R. M. "The Fictive Uses of Language." *Philosophy* 46 (1971): 324–40.

George, K. *Rhythm in Drama.* Pittsburgh: University of Pittsburgh Press, 1980.

Ginestier, P. *Vers une science de la littérature: Esthétique des situations dramatiques.* Paris: Presses Universitaires de France, 1961.

Helbo, A., ed. *Sémiologie de la représentation.* Brussels: Editions Complexe, 1975.

Helbo, A., *Les Mots et les gestes, essai sur le théâtre.* Lille: Presses Universitaires de Lille, 1983.

Hess-Lüttich, E. "Drama, Silence and Semiotics." *Kodikas* 1, no. 3 (1979); 199–215.

———. "Towards a Semiotics of Discourse in Drama." *Kodikas/Ars Semeiotica* 6, no. 3–4 (1983): 187–201.

Honzl, J. "Dynamics of the Sign in the Theater" (1940). In *Semiotics of Art,* edited by L. Matejka and I. Titunik. Cambridge, Mass.: MIT Press, 1976.

Ingarden, R. "The Functions of Language in the Theatre," in *The Literary Work of Art,* translated by G. Grabowicz. Evanston, Ill.: Northwestern University Press, 1973, 377–96.

Issacharoff, M. "Space and Reference in Drama." *Poetics Today* 2, no. 3 (1981): 211–24.

———. "Texte théâtral et didascalecture." *MLN* 96, no. 4 (1981): 809–23.

———. *Le Spectacle du discours.* Paris: José Corti, 1985.

———. "Inscribed Performance." *Rivista di Letterature Moderne e Comparate* 35, no. 2 (1986): 93–105.

———. "Comic Space." In *The Theatrical Space.* Cambridge: Cambridge University Press, 1986, 187–98.

———. "How Playscripts Refer: Some Preliminary Considerations." In *On Referring in Literature,* edited by A. Whiteside and M. Issacharoff. Bloomington: Indiana University Press, 1987.

Jacquot, J., and Bablet, D., eds. *Le Lieu théâtral dans la société moderne.* Paris: Editions du CNRS, 1963.

Kelsey, R. "The Actor's Representation: Gesture, Play and Language." *Philosophy and Literature* 8, no. 1 (1984): 67–74.

Kennedy, A. *Dramatic Dialogue*. Cambridge: Cambridge University Press, 1983.

Kerbrat-Orecchioni, C. "Le dialogue théâtral." In *Mélanges de Langue et de Littérature Française offerts à Pierre Larthomas*. Paris: Ecole Normale Supérieure de Jeunes Filles, 1985, 235–49.

Konigson, E. *L'Espace théâtral médiéval*. Paris: Editions du CNRS, 1975.

Kowzan, T. *Littérature et spectacle*. Paris: Mouton, 1975.

————. "Le spectacle, lieu de rencontre privilégié entre la littérature, les arts plastiques et la musique." *Semiotica* 44, nos. 3–4 (1983): 297–305.

————. "Iconographie-iconologie théâtrale: Le signe iconique et son référent." *Diogène* 130 (1985): 51–68.

————. "Avant-garde, modernité, créativité: Jeu insolite entre signifiants, signifiés et référents au théâtre." *Semiotica* 59, no. 1–2 (1986): 69–91.

Krysinski, W. "Semiotic Modalities of the Body in Modern Theater." *Poetics Today* 2, no. 3 (1981): 141–61.

————. Poland of Nowhere, the Breasts of Tiresias and Other Incongruities or Referential Manipulation in Modern Drama." In *On Referring in Literature*, edited by A. Whiteside and M. Issacharoff. Bloomington: Indiana University Press, 1987.

Larthomas, P. *Le Langage dramatique*. Paris: Armand Colin, 1972.

————. "Image verbale et représentation." *Travaux de Linguistique et de Littérature* 19, no. 2 (1981): 153–60.

Lemarinel, J. "Reflexions sur les problèmes méthodologiques spécifiques au théâtre." *Papers on Seventeenth Century French Literature*, 1985, 35–42.

Literature in Performance 3, no. 2 (1983).

Marinis, M. de. "Lo spettacolo come testo I." *Versus* 21 (1978): 66–104.

————. "Lo Spettaculo come testo II." *Versus* 22 (1979): 3–31.

————. *Semiotica del teatro: l'analisi testuale dello spettacolo*. Milan: Bompiani, 1982.

Martin, J. "Ostension et communication théâtrale." *Littérature* 53 (1984): 119–26.

Matejka, L., and Titunik, I., eds. *Semiotics of Art*. Cambridge, Mass.: MIT Press, 1976.

Modern Drama 1982 (Special Issue: Theory of Drama and Performance). 25, no. 1.

Molinari, C., and Ottolenghi, V. *Leggere il teatro*. Florence: Vallecchi, 1979.

Mukarovsky, J. *The Word and Verbal Art (Selected Essays)*. Translated and edited by J. Burbank and P. Steiner. New Haven: Yale University Press, 1977.

————. *Structure, Sign and Function (Selected Essays)*. Translated and edited by J. Burbank and P. Steiner. New Haven: Yale University Press, 1978.

New Literary History 11, no. 3 (1971) (Performance in Drama, the Arts and Society).

Bibliography

Orr, J. *Tragic Drama and Modern Society: Studies in the Social and Literary Theory of Drama from 1870 to the present.* London: Macmillan, 1981.

Pavis, P. "Problèmes d'une sémiologie du théâtre." *Semiotica* 15, no. 3 (1975): 241–63.

———. "Théorie du théâtre et sémiologie: sphère de l'objet et sphère de l'homme." *Semiotica* 16, no. 1 (1976): 45–66.

———. "Problems of a Semiotics of the Theatrical Gesture." *Poetics Today* 2, no. 3 (1981): 65–93.

———. *Languages of the Stage.* New York: Performing Arts, 1982.

———. *Voix et images de la scène. Pour une sémiologie de la réception.* Lille: Presses Universitaires de Lille, 1985.

———. *Dictionnaire du théâtre,* 2d ed. Paris: Editions sociales, 1987.

Pfister, M. *Das Drama: Theorie und Analyse.* Munich: Fink, 1977.

Poetics 13, no. 1–2 (1984) (Special Issue: The Formal Study of Drama, edited by S. Marcus).

Poetics Today 2, no. 3 (1981) (Drama, Theater, Performance. A Semiotic Perspective).

Polieri, J. *Scénographie, sémiographie.* Paris: Denoël/Gonthier, 1971.

———. *Jeu(x) de communication: Recherches—Eléments théoriques.* Paris: Denoël/Gonthier, 1981.

Redmond, J., ed. *The Theatrical Space.* Cambridge: Cambridge University Press, 1987.

Rozik, E. "Theatre as a Language: A Semiotic Approach. *Semiotica* 45, no. 1–2 (1983): 65–87.

Ruffini, F. "Semiotica del teatro: per un'epistemologia degli studi teatrali." *Biblioteca Teatrale* 14 (1976): 1–27.

———. *Semiotica del testo: l'esempio teatro.* Rome: Bulzoni, 1978.

Saison, M. "Les Objets dans la création théâtrale." *Revue de Métaphysique et de Morale* 79, no. 2 (1974): 253–68.

Savona, J. "Narration et actes de parole dans le texte dramatique." *Etudes Littéraires* 13, no. 3 (1980): 471–94.

Schechner, R. *Public Domain.* New York: Bobbs-Merrill, 1969.

———. "Drama, Script, Theatre and Performance." *TDR* 17, no. 3 (1973): 5–36.

———. *Environmental Theatre.* New York: Hawthorn Books, 1973.

———. *Essays on Performance Theory, 1970–1976.* New York: Drama Book Specialists, 1977.

———. *Between Theater and Anthropology.* Philadelphia: University of Pennsylvania Press, 1985.

Schechner, R., and Schuman, M., eds. *Ritual, Play, and Performance.* New York: Seabury Press, 1976.

Schmeling, M. *Métatexte et intertexte: aspects du théâtre dans le théâtre,* Paris: Minard (*Archives des Lettres Modernes* No. 204), 1982.

Schmid, H., and Van Kesteren, A. *Semiotics of Drama and Theatre.* Amsterdam: Benjamins, 1984.

Searle, J. "The Logical Status of Fictional Discourse." *New Literary History* 6:319–32. (reprinted in Searle, *Expression and Meaning,* Cambridge: Cambridge University Press, 1979).

Segre, C. "A Contribution to the Semiotics of Theater." *Poetics Today* 1, no. 3 (1980): 39–48.

Semiotica 47, no. 1–4 (1983) (Special Issue: Puppets, Masks and Performing Objects from Semiotic Perspectives, edited by F. Proschan).

Serpieri, A., *Come comunica il teatro: dal testo alla scena.* Milan: Il Formichiere, 1978.

Short, M. H. "Discourse Analysis and the Analysis of Drama." *Applied Linguistics,* 11, no. 2 (1981): 181–202.

Souriau, E. *Les Deux cent mille situations dramatiques.* Paris: Flammarion, 1950.

———. "Le cube et la sphère." In *Architecture et dramaturgie.* Paris: Flammarion, 1950, 63–83.

States, B. *Irony and Drama: A Poetics.* Ithaca: Cornell University Press, 1971.

———. *Great Reckonings in Little Rooms: On the Phenomenology of Theatre.* Berkeley: University of California Press, 1985.

Styan, J. *The Dramatic Experience,* Cambridge: Cambridge University Press, 1965.

———. *Drama, Stage and Audience.* Cambridge: Cambridge University Press, 1975.

———. *Modern Drama in Theory and Practice.* Cambridge: Cambridge University Press, 1981.

Thomasseau, J-M. 1984 "Les différents états du texte théâtral." *Pratiques* 41 (1984): 99–121.

Tomasino, R., ed. *Semiotica della rappresentazione.* Palermo: Flaccovio, 1984.

Tonelli, F., and Hubert, J. "Theatricality: The Burden of the Text." *SubStance* 71 (1978): 79–102.

Turner, V. *Dramas, Fields, and Metaphors.* Ithaca, N.Y.: Cornell University Press, 1974.

———. *From Ritual to Theatre: The Human Seriousness of Play.* New York: Performing Arts Journal Publications, 1982.

Ubersfeld, A. *Lire le théâtre.* Paris: Editions sociales, 1977.

———. *L'Ecole du spectateur.* Paris: Editions sociales, 1981.

Urmson, J. O. "Dramatic Representation." *Philosophical Quarterly* 22, no. 89 (1972): 333–43.

Veltrusky, J. "Dramatic Text as a Component of Theatre." In *Semiotics of Art,* edited by L. Matejka and I. Titunik. Cambridge, Mass.: MIT Press, 1976, 94–117.

———. *Drama as Literature.* Lisse: Peter de Ridder Press, 1977.

Versus 21 (1978) (Teatro e semiotica, edited by M. de Marinis).

Bibliography

Versus 22 (1979) (Teatro e communicazione gestuale).

Wiles, T. *The Theater Event: Modern Theories of Performance.* Chicago: University of Chicago Press, 1980.

Wilson, E. *The Theater Experience.* New York: McGraw-Hill, 1980.

Zich, O. *Estetika dramatického umeni* (Aesthetics of dramatic art). Prague: Melantrich, 1931.

Zuber, O. *The Languages of Theatre: Problems in the Translation and Transposition of Drama.* Oxford: Pergamon Press, 1980.

Contributors

JEAN ALTER, Professor of Romance Languages, University of Pennsylvania, is the author of *La Vision du monde d'Alain Robbe-Grillet, Les Origines de la satire anti-bourgeoise* and *L'Esprit anti-bourgeois sous l'ancien régime.* He is founding editor of *Forum,* an international newsletter for the semiotics of theatre.

KEIR ELAM is Ricercatore in English at the University of Florence and author of *The Semiotics of Theatre and Drama* and *Shakespeare's Universe of Discourse. Language-Games in the Comedies.*

MICHAEL ISSACHAROFF is Professor of French at the University of Western Ontario. His most recent books include *L'Espace et la nouvelle* and *Le Spectacle du discours.* He is editor of *Langages de Flaubert* and coeditor of *Sartre et la mise en signe* and *On Referring in Literature.* His *Discourse as Performance* is soon to be published by Stanford University Press.

ROBIN F. JONES, Associate Professor of French at the University of Western Ontario, is coeditor of *The Nature of Medieval Narrative* and editor of several Anglo-Norman homelitic and culinary texts. He has also written on reception theory and is currently preparing an edition of *La Novele Cirurgerie.*

PATRICE PAVIS is Maître de Conférences at the Institut d'Etudes Théâtrales, Université de Paris III. He is author of *Problèmes de sémiologie théâtrale, Voix et images de la scène, Dictionnaire du théâtre,* and *Marivaux à l'épreuve de la scène.*

RICHARD SCHECHNER is Professor of Performance Studies at New York University/Tisch School of the Arts. He is editor of *The Drama Review.* His most recent books include *Environmental Theatre, Essays on Performance Theory,* and *Between Theatre and Anthroplogy.* His most recent theatre work includes *Prometheus Project,* after Aeschlylus, and *Don Juan,* in his own translation from Molière's French.

J. L. STYAN is the Franklyn Bliss Snyder Professor of English Literature and Professor of Theatre at Northwestern University. He has published some one hundred articles and fifteen books on the theory and practice of drama, the most recent being *Restoration Comedy in Performance.*

Contributors

ANNA WHITESIDE is Associate Professor of French and Comparative Literature at McMaster University. She is coeditor of *On Referring in Literature* and author of numerous articles on literary theory. She is currently writing a book on Apollinaire and visual poetics.

Index

Abel, L., 17, 26
Adams, H., 58
Alter, J., 1, 7, 85, 140, 153
Althusser, L., 28
Anouilh, J., 28
Apollinaire, G., 35–36
Appia, A., 98
Aristotle, 2, 4, 41, 42, 47, 48, 49, 50, 51, 54, 55, 56, 77
Artaud, A., 4, 51, 58, 140, 142
Austin, J. L., 4, 40, 41, 42, 45, 47, 50, 51, 56, 57, 58, 141, 142

Balzac, H. de, 59
Barthes, R., 2, 4, 5, 48, 49, 57, 59, 60, 61, 65, 73
Beckett, S., 5, 11, 23, 62, 66, 67, 68, 69, 70, 71, 74, 139
Benveniste, E., 63, 72, 73, 74, 114
Bloom, H., 143
Bogatyrev, P., 2
Borges, J. L., 62, 63, 73
Boulez, P., 1
Braun, E., 26
Brecht, B., 23, 25, 46, 49, 50, 54, 55, 58, 88, 97
Bresson, R., 28
Brook, P., 98
Brown, J. R., 9
Brusak, K., 2
Burbank, J., 100

Castelvetro, L., 51, 54, 55, 58
Chambers, R., 46, 47, 57
Chatman, S., 57
Chekhov, A., 13, 23, 24
Chéreau, P., 90, 92, 96

Chomsky, N., 41
Cocteau, J., 30–31, 32, 33, 35, 37
Cohen, G., 114
Coleridge, S. T., 51, 55, 58
Copeau, J., 12
Craig, G., 89, 98
Culler, J., 60, 73

Derrida, J., 140, 141, 142
Dodd, W., 57
Donleavy, J. P., 63, 64, 65, 73
Donnellan, K., 26, 27, 36
Dryden, J., 13, 26, 41, 56
Dubois, J., 72
Duras, M., 35

Eco, U., 62, 72
Elam, K., 1, 2, 3, 4, 5, 6, 9, 12, 26, 27, 36, 57, 61, 73, 76, 85, 102, 114, 140, 153
Eliot, T. S., 18

Flaubert, G., 1, 76, 77
Fowlie, W., 26
Frank, G., 105, 114, 115
Freud, S., 91
Fuchs, G., 54, 58

Gale, R. M., 57
Galsworthy, J., 44, 45
Garrick, D., 18, 46
Genet, J., 23, 25, 31, 37, 62, 67
Gielgud, J., 45
Giraudoux, J., 14, 28, 30, 33, 36
Goethe, J., 101
Goldsmith, O., 22, 26
Grabowicz, G., 100
Grass, K., 114

Index

Greisenegger, W., 114
Grotowski, J., 135
Gunderson, K., 57
Guthrie, T., 14

Handke, P., 24
Hartman, G., 139–40, 142
Hollingshed, J., 23
Honzl, J., 2
Horace, 4, 49, 54, 58
Hugo, V., 78

Ibsen, H., 13, 20, 24
Ingarden, R., 88, 93, 100
Ionesco, E., 8, 28, 29, 36, 63, 65, 66, 73
Irving, H., 18
Ishii, M., 7
Issacharoff, M., 1, 5, 37, 73, 74, 85, 100, 102, 103, 114, 140, 143, 153

Jakobson, R., 59, 63, 72
Jarry, A., 24
Johnson, S., 11, 12, 13, 15, 26
Jones, R. F., 1, 5, 6, 7, 140, 153

Kemble, J., 46
Kernodle, G., 110
Koestler, A., 48
Konigson, E., 110, 111, 114, 115
Kowzan, T., 61, 73, 76, 85
Krysinski, W., 37

Lardner, R., 63, 64, 73
Lassalle, J., 89, 90, 96
Lazarowicz, K., 13
Levin, S. R., 56
Linsky, L., 36
Lyons, J., 26, 27, 36

Maeterlinck, M., 14
Marinis, M. de, 57
Marivaux, P., 4, 87, 88, 89, 90, 96
Matejka, L., 85
Mathieu, M., 114
Maugham, S., 45
McConaachie, B., 115
McDougall, G., 7
Mesguich, D., 90
Mayerhold, V., 14
Miller, J. H., 143
Mnouchkine, A., 7, 8, 75, 80, 81, 82, 83, 84

Molière, 30, 32, 33, 37
Montgomery, R. L., 58
Morgan, W., 115
Morris, C., 40, 41, 46, 56
Muir, L., 109, 115
Mukarovsky, J., 2, 88, 98, 100

Noomen, W., 106, 115
Norris, C., 140, 142

Obaldia, R. de, 66
Ogden, C. K., 36
Ohmann, R., 42, 57
Olivier, L., 45, 77, 78

Painter, M. T., 126, 136
Passow, W., 11, 15, 26
Pavis, P., 1, 3, 4, 5, 6, 8, 9, 11, 26, 77, 100, 140, 153
Pinter, H., 23, 36, 66
Pirandello, L., 17, 23, 24, 25, 30, 33, 42, 57
Piscator, E., 25, 26
Pitoëff, G., 24
Planchon, R., 100
Plato, 95
Prague School, 2, 76

Rabkin, N., 9, 26
Racine, J., 10
Raleigh, W., 26
Raysor, T. M., 58
Reinhardt, M., 25
Resnais, A., 35, 38
Richards, I. A., 36
Riffaterre, M., 60, 61, 73
Righter, A., 14, 20, 26
Robbe-Grillet, A., 35
Ruffini, F., 57
Russell, B., 36

Saint-Simon, 32
Saporta, M., 1
Sartre, J. P., 5, 70
Saussure, F. de, 141
Savona, J., 57
Scaliger, J. C., 4, 41, 43, 44, 49, 54, 55, 56
Schechner, R., 1, 6, 7, 135–36, 137, 140, 153
Searle, J., 3, 26, 27, 36, 40, 42, 43, 44, 45, 46, 50, 57, 58, 89, 100, 142

Index

Sebeok, T., 72
Serpieri, A., 57
Shaffer, P., 31
Shakespeare, W., 5, 7, 9, 10, 12, 13, 16, 17, 18, 19, 20, 23, 26, 39–40, 42, 43, 45, 56, 76, 78, 80, 81, 82, 83, 84, 139, 140, 141, 142
Shaw, G. B., 28, 42, 45, 62
Sherson, E., 26
Short, M. H., 57
Sidney, P., 4, 43, 4, 47, 48, 49, 54, 57, 58
Singh, V. N., 120, 123
Spicer, E. H., 126, 128, 130, 132, 134, 136–37
Stanislavski, K., 46, 97
Steiner, P., 100
Stoppard, T., 24, 29, 66
Strawson, P. F., 26, 27
Strehler, G., 100
Studer, P., 114
Styan, J., 1, 2, 3, 26, 91, 100, 140, 153

Tardieu, J., 33–34, 66, 69, 74
Taylor, E., 46

Thomas, D, 65, 66, 67, 73
Titunik, I., 85
Tulsidas, 117

Ubersfeld, A., 2, 5, 27, 36, 57
Urmson, J., 57

Valmiki, 117
Veltrusky, J., 2
Vinaver, M., 98
Vitez, A., 84, 91, 98, 100
Voltaire, 69

Ward, W. C., 26
Weiss, P., 24
Wellek, R., 59
Whiteside, A., 1, 8, 37, 85, 100, 140, 154
Wickham, E. C., 58
Wilde, O., 13
Wordsworth, W., 10
Wycherley, W., 21, 26

Zich, O., 2
Zumthor, P., 102, 114